Dear Mike & Beri,

Happy Cooking,

Love,

Cori Levi

April 2008.

the good enough to eat®
BREAKFAST
COOKBOOK

Carrie Levin
with William Perley

WARNER BOOKS

An AOL Time Warner Company

Warner Books, Inc., 1271 Avenue of the Americas, New York, NY 10020
Visit our Web site at www.twbookmark.com

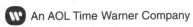 An AOL Time Warner Company

Printed in the United States of America

First Printing: September 2001
10 9 8 7 6 5 4 3 2 1

Library of Congress Cataloging-in-Publication Data

Levin, Carrie.
    The Good Enough to Eat Breakfast Cookbook / Carrie Levin, with William Perley.
        p. cm.
    Includes index.
    ISBN 0-446-52826-9
    1. Breakfasts. 2. Cookery, American. I. Perley, William. II. Good Enough to Eat, Inc.
(Manhattan, New York, N.Y.) III. Title.
TX733 .L48 2001
641.5'2—dc21   2001017541

Illustrations by William Perley,
with thanks to Abby Carter

Book design and text composition by L&G McRee

To Goo-goo and Noo-noo, who only re-heat.

◆◆◆◆◆ ACKNOWLEDGMENTS ◆◆◆◆◆

Gratitude to all those who are or once were a part of the staff at Good Enough to Eat over the last twenty years; to Lester-Lobster who makes everything pretty; to customers who come back year after year and keep me on my toes; to Arthur Leeds and his family for a roof over our heads; to brother Doug, the juice wizard; to Bill Malloy for getting us going; to Caryn Karmatz-Rudy and Sandra Bark for keeping us going; to the best Bests next-door Sarah Black, Norman Marshall, and Miguel Medina; to Mark for the legal stuff; to Amy's bread; to Gurumayi Chidvilasananda for reminding me what's important; to my sons, Bucko, Asa, and Conner, for putting up with their overworked mom; and to my husband, Bill, who knows how to put me into words.

✦✦✦✦✦✦✦✦ CONTENTS ✦✦✦✦✦✦✦✦

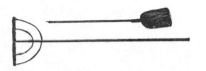

Dear Reader:

Nota bene: This is not a book for the coffee table. Nothing is on the plate just for decoration and no ingredient is listed because it is artsy or *en vogue.* If I want you to use "freshly ground black pepper," I'll say so. I have written *The Good Enough to Eat Breakfast Book* to be useful, and I hope it becomes the most page-worn book in your kitchen.

I wrote my thesis on eggs at the Leith School of Food and Wine in London when I was nineteen years old. Twenty-four years later and after twenty years of being the chef and owner of Good Enough to Eat, I think I have achieved a sort of graduate degree in omelettes and, in fact, everything else that goes on the breakfast table. I know that sounds immodest, but if the proof is in the pudding, the success of breakfast at Good Enough is that proof.

These recipes work. They were arrived at through years of trial and error and feedback from thousands of customers at the restaurant. There are also a lot of details on the techniques to be used in preparation. Because of this, some of the recipes may seem a little long or complicated. But . . . a simple list of ingredients and a pretty picture is not enough to produce optimum results. You need to know the tricks. I've learned a lot of them. They make a big difference, and I gladly share them with you.

A number of loyal customers have said to me, "How can you give away your recipes, your secrets? Everyone will open a Good Enough to Eat!" Well, in answer to that, a number of restaurants have opened using my first cookbook, researching my place, and copying my menus. Some of these establishments have even achieved a certain measure of success. Some of the cooks I have trained have become chefs or opened their own places. I might have gotten my back up now and then over this effort to clone my success, but *c'est la vie*. Imitation is the sincerest form of flattery, right?

Food is personal. What we eat, cook, and serve reflects our character, conviction, and taste. The purpose of this book is to guide you to a result that I would like you to arrive at. Of course, all recipes have evolved from earlier recipes—these included. Try them my way to begin with, and then play with them, make them your own, be creative. That's the way I developed them. Taste is like a fingerprint—there's an infinite variety.

Finally, food is meant to be shared. A recipe may be written to "serve one," but it is always the case that you are cooking for someone you care about, whether it be yourself, friend, family, or customer. This book is my way of sharing something I love with you. I hope you will share it with many others.

Okay, there's the alarm! It's time to wake up and make something "good enough to eat." Have fun!

Love,

Carrie

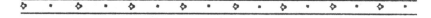

ONE

What's in the Kitchen?

One of my customers at the restaurant says that all he has in his kitchen at home is juice and white wine—he eats all his meals at Good Enough to Eat! Well, that's fine for my business but not for those of us who cook at home. Here are suggestions for what I think you need to have on hand in your kitchen. I'm assuming that you have the basics: salt and black pepper for the shakers, granulated white sugar, baking soda and baking powder.

Spices: Make sure they're fresh; if they sit too long on the shelf, they get bitter.

    Cayenne pepper
    Red pepper flakes
    Cinnamon (sticks and ground)
    Cloves (whole and ground)
    Allspice
    Cracked black pepper
    Kosher salt

Near my stove at home I keep salt and pepper mixed together, red pepper flakes, and baking soda (for blanching vegetables) in little glazed ceramic pots my children made at school. It's also good to keep olive oil, vegetable oil (I use canola), and red wine vinegar close at hand.

Flour and grains:
　　All-purpose flour: any brand, but never "self-rising"
　　Buckwheat flour
　　Whole-wheat flour
　　Cornmeal: yellow, coarsely ground
　　Spelt: light spelt only
　　Cracked wheat
　　Wheat germ: toasted (refrigerate after opening)[*]
　　Grits
　　Oatmeal: regular, not the instant variety

Nuts and seeds:
　　Pumpkin seeds (toasted and raw)
　　Sunflower seeds (toasted and raw)
　　Walnuts
　　Cashews
　　Pecans

Cocoa: Higher grades contain less sugar and are richer in cocoa. I prefer Callebaut.

Honey: Never cook or heat honey.

Maple syrup: There's no substitute for the real thing!

Pectin: You can buy it at the store. I'll also tell you about natural sources.

Sugar:
　　Dark brown: Once opened, it can quickly dry into a hard
　　　　brick; reseal it well or put it in a tight canister with a
　　　　piece of apple to keep it moist.

---

[*]Wheat germ is the only grain, flour, or cereal (that I know of) that needs to be refrigerated, because the oil in the germ can become rancid. Store flours and grains in well-sealed containers in a dry place.

Confectioners' sugar: For icings; keep a couple one-
pound boxes in the cupboard.
Brown cubes or sugar-in-the-raw: The cubes for coffee
remind me of Europe.
Granulated white sugar.

Yeast: Dry or fresh. It's probably easier to work with dry yeast
at home.

Vanilla extract: Pure.

Vegetable shortening: Such as Crisco.

In the refrigerator:
Butter: Unsalted, as white as possible.
Milk: We use a milk with lowered fat content for our
coffee at home, but whole milk should be used for baking.
Buttermilk: Gets thicker as it gets older, and in these
recipes, thicker is better. It will keep in the refrigerator
for about two weeks (after all, it's already curdled!).
Sour cream: Whole-milk variety.
Yogurt: Whole-milk, with acidophilus.
Eggs: These recipes call for large size fresh eggs.
Ginger: Fresh root.
Lemons: With tight, not too thick, skins. Always have
them on hand for juice and zest. Lemons can be used
to cut a too-salty taste; the juice brings out flavors and
can substitute for baking soda in blanching.
Parsley: Curly or flat. The curly variety is a little tougher,
greener, and harder to clean than the flat. Store in the
crisper and clean only when ready to use.
Basil: Freshly picked if possible—watch out for any bad
leaves.

Fruits: Have seasonal fruits on hand. Keep apples separate
from other fruits, as they will cause other fruits to ripen. Of
course, if you want to make a banana bread the next day, put
the bananas in a bag with an apple overnight.

Equipment:

Biscuit and cookie cutters.

Jelly bags: Cotton drawstring bags used to hold pectin-producing fruits in jelly making. You can buy them in kitchen supply shops or you can make your own with cheesecloth.

Kitchen towels.

Knives: Chef's knife for chopping, and a paring knife. The chef's knife should feel comfortable in your hand.

Mixers: I use a KitchenAid standing mixer. You could use a food processor. A blender will be needed for smoothies.

Oven mitts.

Pans: Large and small. A good-quality, heavy-bottom French omelette pan, properly seasoned (see p. 7), will be invaluable.

Peeler: You can sharpen the blades by peeling raw potatoes!

Pots: Along with the usual assortment of quality pots, you should have an 8-quart stock pot.

Rolling pins: I got used to the French kind (a wooden cylinder tapered at the ends), but any normal-size wooden roller will do. Never put them in water.

Scale: For serious baking and cooking.

Spatulas: Rubber for scraping bowls; metal for turning pancakes.

Stove top and oven: Of course you have one, but the best will allow you to go from very high to very low heat quickly (gas is preferable), and your oven should be accurately calibrated.

Thermometers: An oven thermometer for baking; a candy thermometer is good for jam making and in heating oil for doughnuts to the proper temperature.

Tongs: The chef's "right hand."

Wire whisk: For beating egg whites, whipping cream, and so on. Buy one that feels comfortable in your hand.

Wooden spoons: I love them; one should be two feet long for the jam making.

TWO

Eggs, Eggs, Eggs

EGGS AND I

I mentioned earlier that I did my thesis on eggs at the Leith School of Food and Wine in London. It was 207 pages long and started with the question, "What came first, the chicken or the egg?" My answer was "The egg."

Eggs are probably as perfect as anything you can find in nature: a perfect aerodynamic shape, loaded with protein and vitamins, and oh, so useful in the kitchen—especially for baking. They're useful for other things as well. Egg whites make a great mask for tightening the pores of the skin after a warm shower. After it dries, rinse it off with cold water. I've also found a mixture of oats and egg whites to be very effective in alleviating the skin rashes my three sons got when they were babies. For our purposes in this book, however, I'll stick to its uses as a food.

First, and most important, eggs need to be fresh. At the restaurant my butcher (yep, he's also my egg man) goes to the market every day and gets me the farm-freshest eggs available. You want to avoid any eggs that have been sitting around for any length of time. It's hard to do this, I know, but a couple of experiments at home will help you in winnowing out the bad eggs from the good ones. When you crack open an egg, there should be very little shattering of the shell. If the membrane on the inside of the egg is thick, it will cause extra chattering, and . . . you've got an old egg! Also, when you plop it into the bowl or frying pan, the yolk of a fresh egg will stay in the middle of the white. It looks very pretty when poached—the yolk high and centered. One last caveat: If you find a cracked egg, throw it away and wash the eggs it came with. There are some serious bacterias that enjoy eating eggs as much as we do.

I have never found any difference in white or brown eggs or in "organic" or nonorganic eggs. I know I'll get arguments on that, but for me, it's the freshness that matters. You can cook with eggs straight from the refrigerator, and cold eggs are easier to separate. If you drop one on the floor, douse it with some salt—you can pick it up in about ten minutes. Yolks can be saved for two days with a little water on top, tightly covered with plastic wrap, and kept in a bowl in the refrigerator. Whites can be saved for a week in the same way but without the water.

Being an egg purist, I'm not a big fan of egg substitutes, but I do keep them on hand at the restaurant for special requests. For those who can't eat eggs, scrambled tofu is different but delicious, and I've included one of my favorite recipes for it. Egg-white omelettes pose special problems. Perhaps you've noticed the *humphs* or groans you get in some restaurants when they are ordered. The waiter is exhaling so heavily because he knows the flack he is going to catch from the kitchen. The reason is that egg whites stick like glue to the pans you cook them in. The pan can't be used again until it is scrubbed clean—and then it should be reseasoned! Now that I've done my groaning, I'll admit that I have included a recipe for an egg-white omelette in this book—using a special pan.

In baking, the uses for eggs are manifold. They are a binding agent, a glaze; they add richness and height to breads and cakes. How you handle eggs in mixing with other ingredients and with heat can affect the outcome of everything you cook with them. Whether they're scrambled, poached, fried, or in an omelette, eggs can be beautiful and delicious— none of that brown-on-the-side rubbery stuff you have to hide under ketchup. I'll be much more specific when we get into the recipes.

SCRAMBLED EGGS AND OMELETTES

Tools and Tricks

The pan. There are pans specifically designed for omelettes. The good ones are made of thick and fairly heavy stainless steel or aluminum. I never use a nonstick pan. We used a particular pan at the restaurant for more than nine years. It had a wooden handle and a low lip (the outer edge) and was quite heavy. The omelettes it produced were amazing. It was reseasoned many times, and we all wore black armbands in the kitchen when it finally gave up the ghost. Since then we have used French omelette pans—only four in twenty years—they are certainly worth the expense.

Seasoning the pan. When you get a new pan, it needs to be seasoned so that the eggs don't stick to the surface. There are two ways to season a pan.

1. Cover the bottom of the pan with salt. Put the pan with the salt on the range top over a fairly high flame. Let it sit over the heat until the salt turns colors (the colors depend on the material of the pan); this usually takes about 20 minutes. Repeat this process a second time, and your pan is ready. If you are cooking at home and you never use an abrasive to clean your pan, your pan will last for years before it needs to be reseasoned. This is the method I use.

2. Cover the bottom of the pan with about ⅛ inch of vegetable oil. Put the pan with the oil over a high heat and let the oil smoke for about 7 minutes. Be careful not to overcook the oil; you should be able to wipe out the excess. After you have discarded the excess oil, put the pan into a 500-degree oven for about 10 minutes. Remember that the handle of the pan will be hot when you take it out of the oven. If you have a pan with a wooden handle, use the first method, for heaven's sake!

Beating the eggs. There's a trick to beating eggs for either scrambled eggs or omelettes. It's all in the "click." During the last couple of months of my pregnancy with my youngest son, Conner, I had to stay at home flat on my back. One afternoon I got a call from my manager saying that there was something different about Manny's omelettes. She said they seemed to be a different color and texture—she couldn't figure it out. My manager was on the restaurant's kitchen phone, and since I was immobilized on the couch at home, I asked her to hold the phone close to Manny the next time he beat some eggs. That's when I heard it: the scraping sound coming from a rapid stirring of the eggs. I don't know the scientific explanation of it, but that way of mixing doesn't produce the best eggs. You need to *beat* the eggs using a front-to-back, up-and-down motion, creating a little whirlpool on its side. The magical *click* is the sound of the fork (a four-tine fork is best) striking the bottom and near side of the 4-cup measuring cup we use to beat the eggs at the restaurant. When Manny got the "click" back, his eggs were perfect.

Clarified butter. There are "impurities" in regular butter that can encourage your eggs to stick to the pan. These include milk solids, salt, and water. Here's how to remove them: Heat a stick of butter in a ½-quart pot over a medium-low heat. As soon as the butter is melted, skim the foam from the top. Continue to simmer the butter for about ten minutes. The excess water will burn off and you will be able to see the bottom of the pot. The result will be about 7 tablespoons of clarified butter. This is the healthiest form of butter, and eggs will not stick to the pan as readily as they do with regular butter. All the eggs at Good Enough are prepared with clarified butter.

Technique for Cooking
Scrambled Eggs

All of the egg recipes in this book are for one serving using three eggs. You could scramble less per serving, but I don't recommend using more.

Pour enough clarified butter into your pan to almost cover the bottom surface of the pan (about 2 teaspoons). Let it heat over a medium-high flame while you beat ("click") the eggs in a cup or bowl. (I use 3 eggs for one order of scrambled at the restaurant.) Dribble a little of the egg from the tines of the fork into the heated butter. If it cooks immediately and the bit slides around a little, it's time to pour in the rest of the egg. Do this carefully, pouring into the middle of the butter so that the egg pushes the butter to the outside edges. The egg will cook at the outside edges almost immediately. With the points of your fork pull the egg from the cooked edge toward the center, at the same time tilting the pan in the direction opposite to the pull, causing the uncooked egg in the center to flow into the opened area of the pan. Make sure you keep the pan over the heat while you do this pulling and tilting around the four points of the compass. With practice you will be able to do it without touching the bottom of the pan with the fork. Scraping the bottom of the pan with the fork will cause the egg to stick. The egg will cook quickly and you should keep it moving throughout the process. There is a measure of artistry in this technique, but it is well worth mastering.

Scrambled eggs made this way look softly rumpled and

have a golden sheen. I have taught my cooks to swirl the eggs once just before plating. The degree of doneness is a matter of preference; I like my eggs *baveuse*, which is a French word connoting runniness—I think it actually means "drooling." At Good Enough an order of scrambled goes out with a dusting of finely chopped parsley, two buttermilk biscuits with strawberry butter, and a slice of orange.

Note: Never add salt, pepper, or milk to scrambled eggs at any point before or during cooking: These ingredients will cause the egg to stick to the pan. Add salt and pepper to taste at the table.

Scrambled Eggs with Mushrooms and Parmesan

Makes 1 serving

You can get a nice intense flavor from mushrooms by pressing them with a wooden spoon or spatula while they are sautéing,— to squeeze the water out of them. To clean the surface of mushrooms before slicing and cooking, rub them with a paper towel dipped in water containing a few drops of lemon juice.

Pinch black pepper
Pinch red pepper flakes
2 teaspoons butter (for mushrooms)
3 to 4 medium button mushrooms, cleaned and sliced
    ¼ inch thick
Pinch salt
2 teaspoons clarified butter (for omelette)
3 eggs
¼ cup coarsely grated Parmesan cheese

In an omelette pan bring the pepper, red pepper flakes, and the 2 teaspoons of regular butter to bubbling over a high heat. Add the mushroom slices and let them cook for 1 minute. You'll see the juice coming out of the mushrooms. Press them down at this stage with a spatula or spoon. As the mushrooms cook, scrape the browning from the pan to incorporate its flavor into the mushrooms. Add salt. It will take about 4 minutes for all the water to evaporate and for the mushrooms to get well browned. Transfer the mushrooms to a small bowl and wipe your pan to remove anything that might have stuck to the surface.

Reheat the pan with the 2 teaspoons of clarified butter.

Follow the technique for beating the eggs (p. 8), and when ready, test the heat of the buttered pan with a dribble of egg. If it coagulates immediately and does not stick, return the mushrooms to the pan and then pour in the eggs. Cook the eggs to the desired doneness by pulling them with a fork and tilting the pan as described on page 9. A moment or so before depanning, sprinkle the Parmesan over the eggs, being careful not to let any get on the surface of the pan.

Slide the eggs from the pan onto a warmed plate and sprinkle them with some finely chopped parsley. Then you might add a slice of orange or a strawberry, a side of bacon or sausage, and some buttermilk biscuits.

Southern Scrambled Eggs

Makes 1 serving

My Mom learned how to make eggs this way from her good friend Mrs. Edmonds, who lives in Georgia. When my brother, Doug, and I were kids, she'd serve them to us with a half grapefruit sprinkled with brown sugar, and some buttered toast. Mrs. Edmonds (according to my mother) says that in the South these eggs are served with wedges of cantaloupe sprinkled with salt.

2 teaspoons clarified butter
3 eggs

Heat the butter in a pan—I don't use my omelette pan for these eggs, to avoid the possibility of the whites sticking. If they do, you have to clean and reseason it.

Break the eggs into a bowl and prick each yolk with a fork, but do not beat them.

Once the butter in the pan begins to bubble, do the dribble test. If the egg dribble cooks immediately and doesn't stick, pour in the eggs. Using a fork, stir them with a swirling motion, trying not to touch the tines of the fork to the bottom of the pan. These eggs have a tendency to stick because the whites cook faster than the yolks and will stick more readily. If they do, use a spatula to get them out of the pan when they're done.

Southern Scrambled Eggs have swirls of yellow and white and a different feel in the mouth when you eat them. Don't forget toast and cantaloupe!

Steak and Eggs

Makes 1 serving

I always think of this as a man's breakfast, ever since my husband made it for us with steak and potatoes left over from a dinner we had the night before. Somehow, it seems very American to me, having grown up in Europe where I had never heard of such a breakfast.

½ baked potato, sliced
5 ounces of steak (we use rib eye at the restaurant)
Butter for the griddle

¼ teaspoon salt
¼ teaspoon black pepper
Pinch paprika
2 tablespoons chopped onion (optional)
Bread for toast
3 eggs for the scrambled
2 teaspoons clarified butter

Preheat the griddle to high heat.

If you have that leftover baked potato, slice it about ¼ inch thick. Slice the steak into strips about 1 inch thick.

Butter the griddle, and when it starts to bubble, throw on the salt, pepper, and paprika, then add the onion, if you want it, and let it cook for 2 minutes before putting on the potato. You can lay the steak strips on another area of the griddle to heat up. After about 1 minute turn the steak and the potato, and give them another minute. Remember that if you're starting with potato and steak that are already cooked, you're basically reheating.

If you're starting with uncooked steak and potato, you essentially cook them in the same way, except for an extra step with the potato. Put the uncooked potato slices in a pot of cold water containing ½ teaspoon of salt and bring to a boil. Reduce the heat and simmer the potato, uncovered, for 15 minutes. Drain the potato well before putting on the griddle.

A minute before you take the steak and potato off the griddle, you can push the toast down and start getting ready for the scrambled eggs:

Beat the eggs—clickety-click—to a nice froth. Heat the clarified butter in your frying pan. The toast should be up now. Put it on a plate and put the steak slices on top, then put the potato slices on the plate next to the steak and toast.

Now back to the frying pan. Do the dribble test. Cook the scrambled eggs as you've learned on page 9.

When the eggs are ready, put them on the plate wherever you can find some room. Put some steak sauce on the meat and you're ready for a "manly" breakfast.

Note: When cooking meat, don't salt it before searing the juices in. Salt pulls the juices out. Salt and pepper after searing.

Tricolor Crispy Nachos with Salsa and Eggs

Makes 1 serving

Juan, *a very fine cook who works at Good Enough, made this dish for me one day, and I loved it. He called it* chilaquiles *and made it with scrambled eggs, but he said that in Mexico it is also made with chicken or pork and a cheese called queso fresco. We use feta cheese at the restaurant for this dish. Juan said it was "close enough."*

The tricolor nachos are used primarily for visual effect. If you can't find the tricolors at your grocery, the plain ones will do just as well—but they're not as pretty!

1 teaspoon vegetable oil
4 tablespoons salsa (see following recipe)
15 tricolor nachos
Pinch salt
Pinch black pepper
3 eggs
2 teaspoons clarified butter
3 ounces feta cheese
2 teaspoons chopped red onion

Preheat oven to 150 degrees.

Heat the oil to medium in your frying pan and add the salsa. Now crumble in the nachos. Cook about 3 minutes, pushing the nachos down with the spatula. Add salt and pepper to taste. I like the nachos a little crispy, but if you want them softer, cover the pan and steam them for a minute. Put the nacho-salsa combination on a plate and keep warm in oven.

Prepare the scrambled eggs according to my instructions (pp. 9 and 10).

When the eggs are ready, slide them onto the nachos and salsa that you were keeping warm and top with crumbled feta and the chopped onion. *Rico!*

Good Enough to Eat Tomato Salsa

Makes 4 cups

This recipe makes enough for thirty-six orders of nacho eggs, and you may not be having that many over for breakfast, but if you're going to make it, you might as well make more than enough. You can always cut the recipe in half or make some Mexican lasagna or use it as a dip.

12 ripe plum tomatoes
3 medium jalapeño peppers
½ medium red onion, finely chopped
2 tablespoons finely chopped cilantro
1 garlic clove, minced
2 teaspoons kosher salt

Bring enough water to cover the tomatoes to a boil in a large pot. Core out the stem area of the tomatoes with a paring knife and make an x slash at the bottom of each tomato. Drop the tomatoes into the boiling water and let them bob around for 10 seconds. Take them out with a slotted spoon and let them cool enough to peel off the skins and discard. After peeling, cut each tomato in half and scoop out the seeds and discard them. Now dice the tomatoes into ¼-inch pieces.

Put the jalapeños under the broiler at a high heat. The skins will blister and blacken in spots—turn them so this is uniform over all areas of the peppers. Remove them when this is accomplished and let them cool enough to peel off the skins, which you discard. Now cut the peppers lengthwise and scoop out the seeds and discard them. (If you like your salsa really hot, leave some seeds in with the peppers.) Dice the peppers to ⅛-inch pieces. Be careful to wash or not reuse anything that has come in contact with the jalapeños!

Combine the tomatoes and jalapeños with the onion, cilantro, garlic, and salt in a large bowl and toss together. If it's too hot when you sample it, add some lemon juice and chopped parsley to calm down the heat.

Scrambled Tofu

Makes 2 servings

Tofu is virtually tasteless, so it will take on the flavors of what-ever herbs or spices you mix with it. I find that the following recipe makes a particularly flavorful dish.

1 tablespoon diced red pepper
1 plum tomato
16 ounces firm tofu
1 tablespoon olive oil
1 tablespoon chopped onion
1 tablespoon sour cream
½ teaspoon kosher salt
¼ teaspoon black pepper
⅛ teaspoon tumeric
1 tablespoon nutritional yeast (optional)
1 tablespoon basil chiffonade, or sliced into thin ribbons
    (optional)

Remove the seeds and inside white ribbing from the red pepper before dicing.

Remove the seeds from the tomato and cut into cubes.

Drain the tofu, rinse twice, squeeze out all the water, and crumble between your fingers into a bowl.

Heat the oil in a frying pan, then add the onion and diced pepper and sauté for 2 minutes. Add the tofu and cook for 5–7 minutes over medium heat to evaporate the remaining water.

Add the sour cream, salt and pepper, yeast (if desired), and tumeric and stir until the yellow color from the tumeric is uniform. Now stir in the tomato. Add the basil at this point, or use it as a decorative (and edible) topping. Serve.

Note: You can make a sandwich of Scrambled Tofu by putting it on some 7-Grain Bread (p. 91) with lettuce and mustard. Also, if you store the Scrambled Tofu in the refrigerator, do so in a glass container, as the tumeric will turn plastic yellow.

OMELETTES

An omelette is prepared using the same technique as for scrambled eggs: three eggs, "clicking," clarified butter, dribble test, pulling and tilting, and so on. The difference is that omelettes incorporate other ingredients, and these call for requisite techniques. But for the basic omelette, you pull until the eggs reach the desired degree of doneness. You plate the eggs by sliding them halfway out of the pan onto the plate. Then, by using the edge of the pan still under the eggs, you fold them into a half circle on the plate.

Vermont Cheddar–Apple Omelette

Makes 1 omelette

This omelette, along with the BLT (also an omelette! see p. 20), has been on the Good Enough to Eat menu from the moment we opened for business—twenty years ago.

2 teaspoons clarified butter
6 slices Granny Smith apple, peeled, thinly sliced
  (¼ to ⅓ of the apple)
3 large eggs
3 ounces sharp white Vermont cheddar, coarsely grated

Heat the butter in an omelette pan over a medium-high heat. Add the apple slices when the butter starts to bubble, and cook them for 30 seconds or so, gently shaking them around in the pan. They should be cooked but still firm enough to retain their shape. Moving the pan so as to distribute the apples evenly, add the beaten eggs (p. 8). Pull the eggs from the edges and tilt the pan using the technique described for cooking scrambled eggs (p. 9). About three pulls are all that should be needed before adding the cheese. Being careful not to let any cheese get on the pan (it will stick), pull the eggs about three more times, cooking to desired doneness.

As with all omelettes, tilt the eggs halfway onto the plate, folding them into a semicircle with the edge of the pan. It helps to use a warm plate, as the omelette will cool quickly. Season with a little salt and pepper and enjoy!

Western Omelette

Makes 1 omelette

This one is familiar to anyone who has ever eaten in a diner anywhere in the United States. My recipe for this old standard was created especially for Dr. Eugene Callender, the pastor of the Manhattan Reformed Community Church in Harlem and one of my favorite people in the world.

2 teaspoons clarified butter
1 tablespoon chopped red onion
1¼ ounces cured ham, cut into strips
1 tablespoon each red and green pepper cut into
    ⅛-inch cubes
¼ cup grated pepper jack cheese (optional)
1 tablespoon cooked corn
3 eggs

Heat the butter in a pan over medium-high heat. Add the onion and let it cook for one minute, then add the ham and the peppers. Cook for another minute.

Having beaten the eggs according to my advice on page 8, pour them into the pan. Pull a couple of times and add the cheese and corn. Cook to desired degree of doneness, pulling and tilting slightly, being careful not to let any of the cheese get on the pan.

Slide the eggs out of the pan onto a warmed plate, flipping into a half circle.

Note: If you like cheese in this omelette, you can substitute your favorite for the pepper jack. Cheddar is good. Little cubes of avocado are also good—put them in when you add the corn.

Smoked Salmon Omelette

Makes 1 omelette

This one is chic. Serve when the in-laws come over for a brunch visit.

1 tablespoon chopped dill
1 tablespoon chives (snipped ¼ inch with scissors)
1 ounce sour cream (about 2 tablespoons)
2 teaspoons clarified butter
1½ ounces or 5 thin strips of smoked salmon
3 eggs

Mix the dill, chives, and sour cream together.

Heat the butter in a pan over medium-high heat. Make sure the butter is hot or the salmon will stick. Slip the salmon slices into the hot butter; shake the pan in a quick, short motion over the heat to make sure the salmon is not sticking. Turn the slices once with tongs and give the pan another quick shake.

Beat the eggs as described on page 8, then carefully pour them into the pan and cook by pulling and tilting as described on page 9, until they reach the desired doneness. Now spread on the sour cream–chive-dill mixture, avoiding the edges of the pan, and fold onto a warmed plate. Serve with toast and Apple Butter (p. 161), and a glass of champagne with a strawberry in it(!).

Bacon-Tomato-Gruyère Omelette

Makes 1 omelette

We always called this a BLT from the time we opened the restaurant. I don't know why—it never had lettuce in it.

2 teaspoons clarified butter
1 ounce (1½ slices) of cooked bacon cut into ½-inch
    pieces
3 eggs
1 ounce (¼ cup) grated Gruyère cheese (don't pack it
    down!)
1 ounce (½ of a small) plum tomato, seeded and cut into
    ¼-inch cubes

After the butter is good and hot in the pan, scatter in the bacon. Shake the pan once to make sure the bacon is not sticking. Now pour in the beaten eggs (as described on p. 8). Tilt and pull a couple of times (see p. 9) and sprinkle in the cheese, keeping it well in the eggs. Pull a couple more times to cook to desired doneness.

Scatter in the tomato pieces, avoiding the edge of the pan. Immediately (almost!) depan the omelette, flipping it into a half circle onto your warmed plate. The tomatoes will be sufficiently warmed by being folded into the omelette at the end of the process and shouldn't be cooked so much as to release their water. Water in the pan will cause sticking.

Note: One day I remarked to Keith, a chef who had been with me for many years, that I always seem to be putting cheese in my omelettes. He said, "An omelette without cheese is like a day without sunshine!"

Spinach-Sausage-Feta Omelette

Makes 1 omelette

2 teaspoons clarified butter
5 to 6 spinach leaves, well washed, stems removed, and
　dried well
1¼ ounces cooked pork sausage (see recipe p. 165)
3 eggs
1 ounce (¼ cup) crumbled feta cheese

Heat the butter in a pan over medium-high heat.

Drop the spinach into the hot butter just long enough to
wilt it, then remove it to a side plate. Now put the cooked
sausage into the pan and cook for a minute, shaking the pan
to make sure it doesn't stick.

Add the eggs, pulling and tilting a couple of times, and
then put the spinach back in, being careful not to let it touch
the sides of the pan. Pull a couple of times more until the eggs
are cooked the way you like them.

Now distribute the feta over the eggs, and as you slide the
eggs from the pan onto a warm plate, fold the eggs into the
half circle of the omelette. The feta will become warm in its
spinach-sausage-egg blanket.

Spinach-Salami-Comté Omelette

Makes 1 omelette

I remember this omelette from early-morning breakfasts my husband, Bill, and I used to have in a twenty-four-hour restaurant in Greenwich Village. It's no longer there, I'm sad to say. They made their omelette with Swiss cheese. Comté is a wonderful Gruyère cheese—very close to Swiss in taste and texture but better, I think, and no holes.

2 teaspoons clarified butter
5 to 6 spinach leaves, well washed, stems removed,
  and dried
3 to 5 slices Genoa salami (or your favorite)
3 eggs
1 ounce (¼ cup) grated Comté cheese

In a frying pan, heat the butter over medium-high heat. Add the spinach long enough to wilt, then remove. Now cook the salami for about one minute, moving the pan over the heat, making sure it doesn't stick.

Remembering the technique for preparing the eggs (p. 8), add them to the pan, and pull the mixture a couple of times. Return the spinach to the pan and pull a couple more times. When the eggs are almost done the way you like them, scatter the grated cheese over the top (avoid getting any on the pan!).

As soon as you've got your last bit of cheese scattered, you're ready to fold the omelette onto a warm plate. Serve with toast or some of those biscuits you've been warming in the oven.

Egg-White Omelette with Tomato, Broccoli, and Smoked Mozzarella

Makes 1 omelette

We don't make egg-white omelettes at the restaurant because egg whites are infamous for sticking to frying pans and slowing kitchen service. This is a kind of soufflé omelette to try at home if you want a high protein–low cholesterol egg dish. I used smoked mozzarella to give some extra texture and flavor.

⅔ cup broccoli florets, blanched
4 egg whites
2 teaspoons clarified butter
6 cherry tomatoes, halved
¼ cup smoked mozzarella cut into ⅛-inch cubes

Blanch the broccoli: Fill a medium-sized pot half full of water, add a pinch of salt and baking soda, and bring to a boil. Drop in the broccoli florets. Once the water returns to a boil, reduce the heat and simmer for 1 minute. Drain the broccoli into a strainer and shock under cold running water until cooled. Shake the water from the florets, spread them on a paper towel, and pat lightly with another towel to dry them.

Cook the omelette: Beat the egg whites until they hold a soft peak.

Heat the butter to medium-high in a frying pan.

When the butter in the pan is hot (starting to bubble), add the broccoli and sauté for about 30 seconds until it and the butter are well heated. Using a rubber spatula, add the egg whites to the pan, pushing them out to the edges of the cooking surface evenly. After about 20 seconds add the tomatoes and cheese, spreading them over the eggs.

At this point the egg whites will have cooked for approximately 1 minute, which should be long enough, as the whites cook faster than a yolk-white mixture. So, you're ready to extricate the omelette from the pan. You will probably need your spatula for assistance in folding the omelette onto the plate and for a little patching, as whites tend to break apart.

Serve with dry toast, a slice of cantaloupe, and black coffee or herbal tea.

EGGS: FRIED, BAKED, POACHED, OR BOILED

Fried Eggs

In all egg recipes, the freshness of the eggs is critical. When you slide the egg from its shell into the hot butter in your pan or on the griddle, the yolk of a fresh egg will stay in the center of the white. If the yolk slides to the edge of the white, the egg isn't fresh. It may not be bad, as in inedible, but it won't taste as good as a fresh egg.

Besides this caveat, how you fry your eggs—sunny-side up, over-easy, runny, or well done—is a matter of how you like them.

Heat the butter in a pan over medium heat until it starts to bubble. Crack the egg on a sharp edge and gently slide the egg into the hot butter. Watch out for shell fragments!

The white will cook faster than the yolk. For over-easy, watch the white closest to the yolk—when it appears to be opaque, turn the egg with your spatula. The egg needs about 1½ minutes on the first side and only 10 seconds or less on the second, depending on how well done you want it. I like my egg yolk to be runny, so I leave the egg on the second side for only a few seconds.

Take the egg out of the pan with your spatula, being careful not to break the yolk. Serve with toast or biscuits, with ham, sausage, or bacon, with a couple of pancakes, or with any combination of these.

Hole-in-the-Bread

Makes 1 serving

I first became acquainted with this whimsical way of serving an egg on the first day of a Weight Watchers diet. I was twelve years old and thought I needed to get skinny. We make it at the restaurant with our own Whole-Wheat Bread (p. 89) and our Glazed Baked Ham (p. 175). It's not for weight watchers anymore!

2 teaspoons butter (not clarified)
2 slices bread, thickly sliced—about ¾ inch
2 slices cured ham, 4 ounces each
2 eggs

Heat the butter in a pan or on a griddle over medium-high heat.

If the bread slices are thick, use a 1½-inch biscuit cutter to create the hole in the center of each slice. The hole has to accommodate the entire egg without overflowing, so if the bread is thin, you may have to make the hole larger.

When the butter is bubbling, put the bread slices on the griddle and "toast" them for 2 minutes on each side. Make sure they don't stick. Place the ham slices on the back of the griddle and heat them on both sides until they are a little crispy at the edges. If you don't have a griddle, you'll have to do this under the broiler or in a separate pan. After the bread is golden brown on both sides, break one of the eggs into a small bowl and gently tip the egg into one of the holes. Repeat with the second egg. Cook for 2 minutes more.

Using the spatula, turn the slices over, being careful not to break the egg yolks. After about 10 seconds, your Hole-in-the-Breads should be over-easy—yolks cooked on top but still runny inside. Of course, cooking time should vary according to how you like your eggs.

Put the ham slices onto a warmed plate and place the Hole-in-the-Breads on top of them, leaving some of the ham showing underneath. Serve.

Baked Eggs in Creamed Spinach

Makes 2 to 3 servings

This may sound kind of strange, but as Sam-I-Am says, "Try them!" The success of this dish depends on how good the creamed spinach is, so I'm going to give you a recipe for really good creamed spinach first.

Creamed Spinach

Makes 2 cups

My chef, Seppi, taught me to noisette the butter (explained in this recipe) for this dish, and it makes a huge difference. In the south of France, where I went to school, they drop a couple of poached eggs onto some stewed vegetables left over from dinner and reheated. They have this with some French bread and coffee for a late breakfast.

2 packages frozen chopped spinach
6 tablespoons butter
1 teaspoon kosher salt
¼ teaspoon black pepper
¼ teaspoon paprika
Pinch of nutmeg
1 cup heavy cream

Defrost the spinach and drain off all the water. You can squeeze the water out with your hands or press it out through a sieve.

Melt the butter in a large frying pan over medium-high heat and add the spices. Cook over medium heat. Stir the mixture with a long wooden spoon. It will bubble and foam. Part the foam with the spoon to see if the butter is browning. It is *noisette* when it turns a nice mahogany color and smells like nuts.

Take the pan off the heat and stir in the cream. The cream should never boil—boiling will cause the cream to curdle. Return to the heat and cook to reduce, stirring constantly. The reduction is ready when you can run a line with your finger down the back of the coated stirring spoon and the channel you create holds its edges.

Now take that spinach that you've squeezed every last drop of water out of and, breaking up the clumps, put it into the cream mixture. Stir over the heat for a couple of minutes, coating all of the spinach. The Creamed Spinach is now ready.

Making the Baked Eggs in Creamed Spinach

2 cups Creamed Spinach
4 eggs
2 tablespoons grated Parmesan cheese

Preheat the oven to 350 degrees.

(If you have two metal-handled crêpe pans, they are ideal for making two separate servings. You could also make both servings together in a small glass baking pan.)

Put one cup of Creamed Spinach in each crêpe pan. (If the spinach isn't hot, heat and stir for about 5 minutes on the stove top.) Make two nestlike indentations in the spinach with the back of a spoon. One at a time, break the eggs into a small bowl and then slide the eggs into their "nests." Put the pans into the oven.

Bake for 15 minutes, more or less, depending on how well done you like your eggs. It's sort of nifty to serve this dish right in the crêpe pan, but that blazing-hot handle is treacherous. I suggest using a dry, well-insulated oven mitt to grasp the handle and slide the spinach and egg onto a plate. It will come right out like a pancake. Sprinkle on some Parmesan and try it with some ham.

Poached Eggs

Makes 1 serving

I made hundreds of these for Oeufs Benedict at the Four Seasons, apprenticing under Seppi Renngli. He taught me the tricks of vinegar and swirling the poaching water, which I pass on to you.

White vinegar—a few drops
Pinch salt
2 eggs

Add a few drops of vinegar and a pinch of salt to at least 2 inches of water and bring to a boil. Crack an egg into a small bowl. Have a slotted spoon and a paper towel handy.

Reduce the heat to bring the water just under a boil—the water will be moving but not bubbling. Holding the bowl with the egg in one hand and the slotted spoon in the other, make a swirl in the water and slide the egg into the swirl. Repeat with the second egg. Let the eggs cook to desired doneness.

Take each egg out of the water with the slotted spoon, catching the excess water with the paper towel under the spoon. Serve immediately on a couple of slices of 7-Grain toast (p. 91), with one or two Turkey Sausage patties (p. 166).

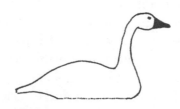

Poached Egg Whites

This is not really a recipe. Instead, it's a trick for satisfying someone who likes poached eggs but is on a serious low-cholesterol diet.

The trick is this: Poach the egg as described above for 5 minutes. The yolk should be cooked through, and after placing it on the plate, scoop out the yolk with a teaspoon and put a strawberry into the void. Pity the poor yolk, and try to give it to someone who's not on a diet.

Boiled Eggs

1 to 2 eggs per serving

There are several theories that I have heard on why hard-boiled eggs get that unsightly purplish-black mantle around the yolks: (1) the eggs weren't fresh to begin with; (2) they sat in the refrigerator too long after they were cooked; (3) they were overcooked. My inclination is to go with theory number 3. Here are two methods of boiling eggs.

2 eggs
White vinegar

1. Place the eggs in a pot large enough to cover them completely with water and still allow an inch or two of splash room at the top. Cover the eggs with cold water and add a few drops of white vinegar. (In case an egg cracks, the vinegar will cause the white to coagulate faster, sealing the egg.)

Bring the water to a boil, and then immediately turn off the heat. Let the eggs sit in the water until it has cooled; the eggs will be nicely hard-boiled and ready for the Easter Bunny.

2. Bring enough water to cover the eggs to a boil in your pot. Gently slip in the eggs and let the water return to a boil. Now reduce the heat so that the water is rolling and the eggs are not banging around in the pot. It will take about 11 minutes for hard-boiled eggs and 3 minutes for soft-boiled.

Note: To peel a hard-boiled egg, roll it on the counter to form a cracked belt down the center. If the egg is fresh, you can easily slide the shell off in two sections.

I like to lop off the top quarter of my soft-boiled egg with a knife, add a little butter and salt and pepper, and scoop the egg out with a spoon. Oh, and have some toast on hand for dunking.

THREE

Pancakes and Blintzes

PANCAKES

The early inspiration for these pancake recipes came from my husband, Bill. I want you to hear the story in his words.

The story of my pancakes (they were blueberry!) goes back to 1980, the first year of our courtship. I had invited Carrie to my NYC sublet on the Lower East Side of Manhattan to have pancakes for breakfast. The invitation came late in the evening of the night before—I had interests in Carrie beyond gastronomy!

The pancakes I made for her that momentous morning started with a box of store-bought mix. It came in a blue box, on the front of which was "Add milk, eggs, and oil." I have never used the "complete—just add water" mixes. Following the directions on the box for amounts, I used eggs for eggs, buttermilk for milk, and a mixture of butter and vegetable oil (3:1) for oil. (If you add a little oil to butter that hasn't been clarified, it won't burn as readily—you don't want burned butter for pancakes.) To the measured portion of dry mix, I threw in two heaping tablespoons of wheat germ.

I was an actor on the road at the time I devised this recipe, and actors always get up late in the morning and have to eat in a hurry and get to rehearsal. Being no exception, I would throw everything together and mix it up rather quickly. My batter looked like a milk shake just pulled off the mixer stem. I found out later from Carrie that overbeating is bad for pancake batter, so in my rush I was getting the right consistency.

My pan was always very hot from cooking bacon beforehand, so after a quick scrape and wipe to remove the bacon fat and stuck-on stuff, I put in a drizzle of reserved butter-oil, got the heat back up, and poured the first pancake. As soon as the batter stopped spreading and the edges rounded up, I distributed some blueberries over the top. When the edges started to show a little color and bubbles appeared in the inner area of the pancake, it was time to flip.

After another minute or so of cooking time, out she came. I turned the pancake blueberry side up on the plate, dropped a few fresh berries on the top, drizzled on some real maple syrup, and added a touch of molasses. I quickly set it down in front of Carrie so that it would be hot from the first bite. Then I stood there and waited to see if I would be considered worth having any more breakfasts with.

My pancakes passed muster and we have shared "breakfast" ever since. A lot of Carrie's pancake recipes have evolved from those blueberry pancakes, and you might say that our sons, Bucko, Asa, and Conner, have "evolved" from them as well.

Mixing

My husband got everything right in the preceding story. There are only a few things I'd like to add about mixing.

1. I recommend a 6-quart glass bowl for mixing the batter.
2. A four-tine fork works nicely for all mixing. You could use a rubber spatula at the end to get out the last of the batter.
3. Put all dry ingredients in your bowl first and mix thoroughly. Then, using the same measuring cup, beat the eggs together with the buttermilk to an even yellow color.
4. Pour the liquid into the dry and mix with your fork. Use a cutting action with the fork and mix until there are no pockets of dry mix left. *Do not beat or overmix the batter.*
5. At this point drizzle in the butter and cut it through the batter. It's all right if a few streaks show in the surface. (I just use regular unsalted melted butter, not clarified, but Bill is right: If you add a little vegetable oil, the butter can be raised to a higher temperature before it burns.)

Now we're ready to cook the pancakes.

Cooking

A well-seasoned griddle is ideal for making pancakes—I can make 6 five-inch cakes at a time on my home griddle—but a good frying pan will do just as well. (Avoid using your omelette pan—it's special!)

The griddle should be preheated medium to medium-high. Play with the heat until you can cook your pancakes about 2 minutes on each side.

Drizzle a little melted butter over the griddle. (You can do this before each batch, but it's not necessary, as some of the butter in the batter will remain on the griddle after you take out the first pancakes.) Now spoon the batter onto the griddle. At home we use a salad spoon with a 3-tablespoon capacity and it produces five-inch pancakes.

Bill's description of what happens to the batter and when to turn the pancake is very good and I recommend you follow it. Ideally you want to turn your pancake only once and *don't pat it with the spatula*. Cooking time should be about 2 minutes on each side, but don't watch the clock—watch the pancake! Once done, the pancakes should be a rich chestnut brown with swirls and craters. If the heat is too low the pancakes will cook too slowly, look an even golden color, and be dry.

4-Grain Pancakes

Makes 13 five-inch pancakes

1½ cups all-purpose flour
2 heaping tablespoons old-fashioned oats
2 heaping tablespoons toasted wheat germ
2 tablespoons* coarse yellow cornmeal
½ teaspoon baking soda
1½ teaspoons baking powder
2 teaspoons sugar
¼ teaspoon salt
2 large eggs
1½ cups buttermilk, or substitute soured milk
   (see p. 35)
¼ cup whole milk (or 2%, 1%, skim)
5 tablespoons melted butter (reserve 1 tablespoon for
   the griddle)

Review techniques for mixing and cooking on pages 33–34.

Preheat griddle to medium or medium-high. Thoroughly mix all dry ingredients. Combine with the beaten eggs, buttermilk, and milk in a bowl, cutting together with a fork. Cut 4 tablespoons of the melted butter into the batter. Drizzle the

---

*All measurements are leveled unless otherwise described.

remaining butter over the griddle and spoon on the batter. The pancakes should cook about 2 minutes per side, but watch them as discussed in Bill's story.

Soured milk: Add 1 tablespoon of sour cream or plain yogurt and 1 tablespoon of fresh lemon juice to 1½ cups whole or 2% milk. Let it sit at room temperature for ½ hour and it will be ready to use—or refrigerate it overnight and use in the morning.

The Diner Stack

Makes 12 pancakes

This is a bare-bones recipe for the kind of pancakes you've had a hundred times at diners all over the country. They usually come to the table stacked like so many oversized silver dollars with a companion peel-top container of artificial maple syrup. I'm sure they started from a box, but . . . who knows? Mine are made from scratch and they are lighter than their multigrain, buttermilk cousins. With some sliced bananas or strawberries on top and real maple syrup and a drizzle of blackstrap molasses for heartiness, they can rival the fanciest flapjacks.

1½ cups all-purpose white flour
2 tablespoons sugar
1 tablespoon baking powder
½ teaspoon salt
2 eggs
1 cup whole or 2% milk
1 teaspoon pure vanilla extract
4 tablespoons butter melted for the batter plus a couple
    more for griddle or pan

Heat the griddle to medium-high.
    Mix the dry ingredients together in a large bowl. Beat the eggs, milk, and vanilla extract in a separate bowl (I use my 2-cup

measuring cup). Pour the liquid portion into the dry, and mix together to the consistency of a thick milk shake. Lastly, cut the melted butter through the batter with a fork. Don't overmix!

Butter the griddle or frying pan, and when it starts to sizzle a bit, spoon on the batter. The butter should not burn, smoke, or turn brown before you put the batter on the griddle. At the moment it becomes transparent, you put on the batter. Follow the technique for cooking discussed on page 33.

If all your pancakes come out exactly the same size and you can stack them with a spatula like rolled coins, you're ready to apply for that job as a breakfast cook at the neighborhood diner.

Apple Pancake with Apple-Raisin Topping

Makes 4 large pancakes

Every summer from the ages of seven to seventeen, I would visit my grandparents at their home in upstate New York. We always had brunch at the same small restaurant, and I always had the same thing—the "German Apple Pancake." Even as a kid I was a kitchen spy, and once I peeked in to watch the woman butter a cast-iron skillet, pour in enough batter to curl up the edges, and press thin slices of apples into the batter. The pancake was served with sour cream and cinnamon-sugar and had a subtle caramel flavor. I loved them. My own Apple Pancake was devised to bring back those happy memories. It has been on my menu for twenty years.

The batter for the Apple Pancake is the same as for the 4-Grain Pancakes (p. 34). I recommend that you make it after you have made the topping, which takes 25 minutes to prepare. Of course, you can serve the pancake with some sour cream and maple syrup (or cinnamon-sugar: 4 teaspoons sugar plus ½ teaspoon cinnamon) and skip the topping if you like.

Note: If you don't make the topping, you will need 1 Granny Smith apple, peeled, cored, and sliced ¼ inch thick for the pancakes.

Apple-Raisin Topping

Makes 2 cups

3 Granny Smith apples—cored, peeled, and cut into
   ½-inch slices
½ cup dark raisins (not the goldens)
1 cup cranapple juice or apple cider
1 tablespoon dark brown sugar (1 additional teaspoon if
   using cranapple juice)
¼ teaspoon ground cloves, allspice, or apple pie spice
¾ teaspoon cinnamon
1 teaspoon fresh lemon juice

Put all ingredients into a 2½-quart pot and bring to a boil. Reduce heat and simmer for 20 minutes. Remove the apple slices and raisins and continue to reduce the liquid until it becomes syrupy—about 5 minutes more. Remove from the heat and restore the fruit to the syrup.

Cooking the Apple Pancake:
   Preheat the griddle and prepare the batter for the 4-Grain Pancakes. Add the butter to the surface of the griddle or frying pan. When the butter is hot (5 to 10 seconds), ladle on enough batter to make a 7- to 8-inch pancake. It takes a little more batter per pancake (6 to 7 tablespoons), but use the back of your ladle or spoon to swirl the surface of the batter to get the diameter.
   Now array the apple slices over the surface of the batter (I do a fan pattern with one slice as a stem). Tap the slices down into the batter with a fingertip so that they are flat and partially covered in batter.
   Cook about 3 minutes, or until golden, and turn. Cook

another 2 minutes. Flip the pancake apple side up onto your plate and serve with a dollop of sour cream, some Apple-Raisin Topping, and some cinnamon-sugar or a little maple syrup. It's the bestest!

Protein Pancakes

Makes 8 pancakes

This recipe comes from my friend Mark, who manages the gym around the corner from the restaurant. It's a weekend special for the bodybuilders and those on low-fat diets. (You have to have a food processor or blender for these pancakes.)

10 egg whites
1 cup oatmeal
1 teaspoon pure vanilla extract
Pinch salt
Pinch cinnamon
No-fat cooking spray (for cooking)

Preheat griddle to medium.

Put everything in the processor and mix well for about 30 seconds.

Spray heated griddle with cooking spray or spray a pan and heat. Spoon on the batter and cook 2 minutes. Turn and cook 1 more minute. As with all pancakes, don't touch or turn more than once—it changes the texture. These pancakes will be a light golden color when done.

Serve with fresh berries and a little powdered sugar.

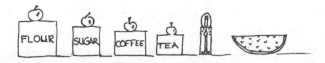

Blueberry Pancakes

Makes 10 five-inch pancakes

Every year in early spring, neighborhood people will stop me on the street and ask if the Blueberry Pancakes are back on the menu. And every year I tell them they're back on after Memorial Day—which is when Good Enough to Eat changes to the summer menu. Blueberries are ideal for pancakes, and as you might guess, they occupy a special place in my heart. We also use sliced strawberries in our Lumber Jill breakfast, which is two strawberry pancakes, two scrambled eggs, and two pork or turkey sausage patties (p. 165–166). Any slightly tart berry will work wonderfully with pancakes, although I don't recommend cooking blackberries or raspberries into the pancake. Just scatter a nice amount on top. The 4-Grain Pancakes batter works beautifully with berries, and it is what we use at the restaurant. The Diner Stack will give you a lighter pancake.

1 pint blueberries (or strawberries, etc.)
4-Grain Pancake batter (p. 34)

Half of the berries will be cooked into the pancakes, and the other half should be saved to scatter over the top of the cooked pancakes for serving.

Butter the heated griddle or pan. Knowing that you're making 10 pancakes, you might want to make a rough estimate of the number of berries you will use for each pancake before starting. Pour the first pancake and distribute the blueberries evenly over the surface. Avoid the extreme edges. Proceed with the next pancake.

If you're using a griddle that will accommodate six or more pancakes, continue this way until you've maxed out the griddle, then return to the first pancake and check it. Each pancake should cook approximately 3 minutes on the first side and 2 minutes on the second.

Arrange the pancakes on your plate, scatter some fresh blueberries over them, and serve with maple syrup.

Note: If a berry should break on the cooking surface and you're going to cook another pancake there, a dribble of water or club soda and a scrape of the spatula will clear it. After all the liquid has evaporated, heat up some more butter and resume cooking.

Banana-Walnut Pancakes

Makes 10 pancakes

Tammi, a screenwriter, tells me that she has figured out that these pancakes contain the full complement of vitamins and minerals that her doctor has recommended she have each day. So, on the late mornings when she comes in, she writes and has her Banana-Walnut Pancakes. They are very satisfying, and if you have them for a late brunch, they will carry you through till dinnertime.

1 cup coarsely chopped walnuts
4-Grain Pancake batter (p. 34)
2 large bananas sliced ¼ inch thick

Half the walnuts will be cooked into the pancakes and half reserved for serving on top.

Preheat the griddle and butter it. Make an estimate of the amount of walnuts you will use for each pancake. Pour the first pancake and distribute the walnuts over the surface. Proceed with the next pancake, and the next, in the same fashion. Return to the first poured pancake and check. Each pancake should cook about 3 minutes on the first side and 2 minutes on the second.

Put the sliced bananas and some walnuts on the finished pancakes and serve with maple syrup.

Note: Don't cook the bananas in the pancakes—they get mushy and gross.

Peter Paul Pancakes

Makes 10 pancakes

The name of these pancakes comes from the famous candy bar. I love the combination of coconut and dark chocolate. We use the Callebaut semisweet dark chocolate tablets and break them up into small, irregular pieces, but chocolate chips will work just fine.

1 cup sweetened shredded coconut
4-Grain Pancake batter (p. 34)
1 cup chocolate in pieces or chips—about 6 ounces

Toast ½ cup of the coconut by spreading it out on a cookie sheet and putting it in a 350-degree oven for about 10 minutes or until golden brown. Shake or move the coconut around with tongs to get even toasting.

Preheat the griddle. Prepare the batter. Portion out the chocolate and coconut for 10 pancakes. (How chocolately or coconutty you want them to be is up to you—experiment, and don't get too anal about the portioning!)

After buttering the griddle, pour the first pancake. Immediately distribute the chocolate and untoasted coconut evenly over the surface. This is done quickly so they will sink into the batter. (Don't mix the chocolate into the batter beforehand!) Proceed to the next pancake, and so on. Go back and check your first pancake. They should cook about 3 minutes on the first side and an additional 2 minutes after turning. Remember my early admonition about not patting the pancakes with the spatula or turning them more than once.

Top the finished Peter Pauls with some toasted coconut and serve with maple syrup.

Stephanie's Swedish Pancakes

Makes 8 nine-inch pancakes

Not too long ago I got a distress call from Jack, one of my Upper West Side customers. He was recently married, and he wanted to give his new wife her favorite breakfast dish, Swedish pancakes, for a surprise birthday brunch. We didn't have them on our menu, so he had been looking all over the city for someone who did. Having had no luck, he was appealing to me for help. I love this sort of thing, so together Jack and I researched and came up with the following recipe.

On June 24, 2000, Stephanie and Jack came to Good Enough to Eat for Stephanie's birthday brunch, and surprise! Stephanie's Swedish Pancakes on the specials menu! She loved them. Jack was very happy, and I was happy to have a new special.

1 cup all-purpose white flour
1 tablespoon sugar
½ teaspoon baking powder
¼ teaspoon baking soda
¼ teaspoon salt
2 eggs
1½ cups 2% milk (powdered milk will also work)
½ cup buttermilk
2 tablespoons butter and ½ teaspoon vegetable oil
    melted together
Additional butter and oil for pan

Preheat oven to 150 degrees for keeping the finished pancakes warm.

Mix all dry ingredients together in a large bowl. Whisk the eggs, milk, and buttermilk together in a separate bowl. Combine the liquid with the dry ingredients in the large bowl. If you have an electric hand blender, it is perfect for this stage of mixing, as you want the silky consistency of a puree. After blending, drizzle in the butter and oil mixture and swirl it through the batter. Now let the batter relax for 5 minutes while you prepare the pan.

A large, well-seasoned, cast-iron frying pan is best. If you don't have one, put it on your Christmas wish list and carry on with the pan you have. Heat the pan to medium-high and brush on some butter-oil. Ladle in about 3 tablespoons (the same amount you would use for a five-inch pancake) and swirl the batter by moving the pan in a counterclockwise direction, keeping the pan over the heat. You can also accomplish the spreading of the batter by swirling the surface with the rounded part of the ladle. Try not to touch the ladle to the bottom of the pan.

Your objective is to move the batter out to the rounded edge of the pan, creating a large, thin pancake. It can be turned when the edges begin to curl and become a little brittle. They need to cook about 2 minutes on both sides. Watch the heat—you may need to adjust it. They should be golden brown when done.

Repeat the process for each pancake. Practice makes perfect! Keep them warm in the oven until you're ready to serve.

Serve these pancakes folded in half with fresh raspberries or strawberries, or Strawberry Jam (p. 154) and sour cream, or any combination of these. Stephanie likes hers with sour cream and lingonberry preserves. Lingonberry preserves can be found at most gourmet food shops.

Buckwheat Pancakes

Makes 36 three-inch pancakes

Jeff and James worked this one out for me. Thanks, boys! An acquired taste is required: They are hearty and sour, good in the winter, and could be served as an hors d'oeuvre with sour cream, smoked salmon, and chives. This recipe takes planning ahead—you have to start the night before.

1 envelope dry yeast
¼ cup warm water (105 to 115 degrees)
1 cup warm buttermilk (105 to 115 degrees)
¾ cup buckwheat flour
½ cup all-purpose white flour
½ cup coarse-grind yellow cornmeal
2 eggs
4 tablespoons molasses
1 tablespoon lemon juice
1½ teaspoons salt
¼ teaspoon baking soda
3 tablespoons melted butter, plus extra for the griddle

In a glass bowl dissolve the yeast in the warm water, stirring with a wooden spoon. Next, stir in the buttermilk, ¼ cup of the buckwheat flour, ¼ cup of the white flour, and ¼ cup of the cornmeal. Cover the bowl with plastic wrap and let it sit on the kitchen counter for 1 hour. It will bubble up. Now add the remaining flours and cornmeal, stir well to mix, then cover with a clean dish towel and refrigerate overnight.

The next morning preheat the griddle to medium-high. Beat the eggs in a bowl and then mix together with the molasses, lemon juice, and salt. The thing that has grown in your refrigerator overnight is called a sponge. Let your sponge out of the fridge and blend the egg mixture into it. Sprinkle the baking soda over the top and blend in. Now stir in the 3 tablespoons butter.

Butter the heated griddle and dollop on the batter. The three-inchers are very good for hors d'oeuvres or noshing. Cook the cakes as you would other pancakes: about 3 minutes on the first side and 2 minutes on the second, with no patting or extra turning.

There are many ways of serving Buckwheat Pancakes. Try them with a spoonful of crème fraîche (p. 189) and a drizzle of honey, or some Chunky Apple Sauce (below), or Apple-Raisin Topping (p. 37) and maple syrup, or as an hors d'ouevre.

Chunky Apple Sauce

Makes 2 cups

2 lbs Granny Smith or McIntosh apples (peeled, cored,
  cut into ¼ -inch chunks)
¼ cup cranapple or apple juice
3 to 4 tablespoons sugar
¾ teaspoon cinnamon

Stir the sugar into the cranapple juice and simmer for about 10 minutes, until sugar is dissolved. Add the apples and stir to coat them. Bring to a boil, then reduce to simmer and cook for 20–25 minutes, stirring frequently.

BLINTZES

Blintzes are the "soul food" of Jewish cuisine. The pancake used to make a blintze is called a bletlach—what the French call a crêpe; the Russians, a blini; the Mexicans, a burrito. A bletlach with a filling rolled in it is called a blintze.

Blintzes can be made with either sweet or savory fillings, but the sweet kind are those traditionally eaten for breakfast.

This recipe was "proven" through a long and historically rich conversation with the grandmother-in-law of my friend Brenda. "Nana," as everyone calls her, didn't have a written recipe, but she explained in detail how bletlachs had been made in her family for generations. Many thanks, Nana!

After the crêpelike pancakes called bletlachs are filled and become blintzes, they can be frozen, and later baked or fried, but *never microwaved*.

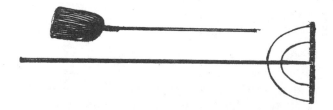

Bletlachs

Makes 20 pancakes

1⅔ cups all-purpose white flour
2 cups plus 2 tablespoons whole or 2% milk
2 eggs
Pinch salt
2 teaspoons vegetable oil for the pan

Put all ingredients except the vegetable oil in a large bowl (6-quart) and mix well. An electric hand blender is very good for achieving the smooth, pureelike consistency you want. Unlike other pancakes for which overbeating is a no-no, this batter should be lump-free. If you don't have a hand blender, press the batter through a sieve with a wooden spoon or rubber spatula. After blending, let the batter rest for 10 minutes.

A crêpe pan, which is made for these pancakes, is about 7½ to 8½ inches in diameter with a little spout to pour off excess batter. If you have a good-quality (by "quality," I mean it conducts the heat evenly) pan of these dimensions, it will serve almost as well.

Have the oil in a small bowl. Dip a small wad of paper towel in the bowl and wipe the surface of the pan, completely coating it with the oil but leaving no excess. Heat the pan to medium. Test the temperature with a dribble of batter—if the batter sets immediately and will slide around in the pan, you're ready to pour the first bletlach.

Remove your tester. (You may need a touch more oil.) Spoon in about 2 tablespoons of batter. Manipulating the pan over the heat, swirl the batter so that it coats the bottom and a little of the side surface of the pan. Once that is accomplished, pour off the excess batter into a handily placed bowl. Your objective is to create the thinnest possible pancake about six inches in diameter. It takes some dexterity, as the process moves quickly.

After 1 minute on the first side, catch the edge of the bletlach with a rubber spatula (or your finger, if you're brave) and flip it. After 30 seconds on the second side, it's done. The finished bletlach might have a slight golden blush, but don't overcook—they should be pliable for rolling in the filling.

Now that you've made the first, move on to the second of the 20 bletlachs you're going to make. Swipe the pan again with the oiled paper towel. You want an even coating of the very least amount of oil. Don't burn yourself! If you've kept the pan over the heat, it should be ready for the next bletlach. Onward to number 20! Once there, we'll make the fillings. Of course, you could have made the fillings first. Whatever!

Cherry Blintze Filling

Makes 2 cups

2 cups pitted sour cherries with their juice
⅓ cup cranberry juice
⅓ cup orange juice
Pinch cinnamon
Pinch ground cloves
Pinch allspice

Chop the cherries in the food processor, but don't liquefy—little chunks are nice.

Bring all ingredients to a boil, then simmer, uncovered, for 45 minutes or until reduced to 2 cups. Remove from heat. Let the filling cool a bit before rolling into the bletlach to make a blintze. This filling can be refrigerated in a covered container for up to 2 weeks.

Cheese Blintze Filling

Makes 2 cups

½ **pound farmer cheese**
½ **pound pot cheese (or ¼ pound cream cheese and**
 ¼ **pound cottage cheese)**
1 **egg**
1 **tablespoon sugar**
1 **teaspoon pure vanilla extract**
½ **teaspoon cinnamon**

Combine the cheeses in the food processor and blend thoroughly. Add the remaining ingredients and pulse together. Transfer to a bowl or container.

It is best to use the Cheese Blintze Filling immediately, since it contains a raw egg. I wouldn't try to save it any longer than 2 days in the refrigerator.

Assemble the blintzes:

Place the bletlach on a flat surface with the second side up (the side of the bletlach that cooked for 30 seconds). Standing directly in front of the bletlach, spoon on about 2 tablespoons of filling to make a log shape slightly off center nearer to you. There should be about an inch of bletlach on either end of the "log."

Fold the sides of the bletlach snugly over the ends of the log, then fold the side of the bletlach near you up and over the log, tucking it as tightly as you can over the far edge of the log. Now roll to complete the blintze.

Cook the blintzes:

Heat some butter in a frying pan over medium heat until it begins to clarify. Think of the blintze as having four sides, and sauté it seam side down first for 1 minute. Repeat on the opposite side for 1 minute, and then on the remaining sides for 1 minute each. Total cooking time is 4 minutes.

You can easily cook four blintzes at a time in your frying pan, and four would make a good number for a single serving.

Savory fillings that are good wrapped into blintzes include Ratatouille (p. 183), Creamed Spinach (p. 26), and practically anything you're using to make omelettes. You could also fold some of your favorite jam into the bletlach and skip the sautéing. Jews (and I'm one of them) would like some sour cream with a hot Cherry Blintze. The French would probably prefer some crème fraîche or powdered sugar and call the blintze a *crêpe*. *Vive la différence!*

FOUR

Waffles and French Toast

WAFFLES

Just as there seem to be people in the world who drink only tea and never touch coffee, so too there are those who prefer waffles to the extent that they never eat pancakes. Perhaps there is some kind of genetic predisposition to one over the other. A waffle person may occasionally switch to an omelette or oatmeal, but never to pancakes.

This is the loosest kind of generality, and I'm sure it will raise a worldwide outcry from its exceptions. However, we all base our expectations on generalities, and attempting to be the exception to the rule can be humorous. I offer the following incident as evidence.

For many years we have had a steady waffle customer named Dave. He would come into the restaurant two or three times a week to have waffles with Orange Butter. Some mornings he would come alone, and occasionally he came with his ten-year-old daughter, Isabel, who would have Strawberry-Almond Waffles. Dave was known to the waiters and waitresses as the waffles-with-orange-butter man.

One morning Dave and Isabel came in and sat down at table six. Lester, the waiter who was covering the table, had already written the order for Dave's waffles when he arrived at the table with a coffee for him and orange juice for Isabel. As Lester was setting the beverages on the table, Dave suddenly said, "I'll have pancakes!" Only that. There was a shocked silence. Isabel stared at her father, who stared at his coffee. Finally, Lester managed to shake off his perplexity and ask, "Pancakes?" Dave nodded in the affirmative and continued to stare. After "I'm still having Strawberry-Almond Waffles," from Isabel, Lester amended his check and departed for the kitchen.

Everything proceeded normally through the O.J. and coffee, and then . . . Lester brought the orders out. He said he felt as though everyone in the dining room was staring at him. The rest of the wait staff certainly was, and the cooks were peeking around the corner from the kitchen.

As Lester tells the story, he placed the three beautiful, hot, sable brown 4-Grain Pancakes with their beaker of maple syrup in front of Dave, and everything stopped. Dave stared at his plate as if he had been turned to stone. Scarcely breathing, Isabel watched her father nervously.

Now, Lester is an artist in his life outside the restaurant, and he is a wonderfully sensitive man. He must have recognized that Dave was in the midst of a crisis of the palate, a sort of gustatory catatonia, from which he could not extricate himself. So after several uncomfortable moments, Lester slid the plate of pancakes out from under Dave's rigid stare and returned them to the kitchen.

A short time later, Lester brought an order of waffles with its ramekin of Orange Butter and slice of orange to Dave, who had been sipping his coffee with a sheepish smile on his face. Isabel hadn't begun to eat. It was as if the pause button on the VCR remote had just been released. Dave dug into his waffles with his usual gusto, and he and his daughter enjoyed an amiable breakfast together. My staff relaxed and went back to work. All was right with the world.

Good Enough to Eat Waffles

Makes 10 waffles

These waffles are a little softer than the toaster types available in the frozen foods section of the grocery store. As they are American in character, they are also thinner, with shallower crevasses, and less sweet than their Belgian and Norwegian cousins. Remember to read carefully the instructions that come with your waffle iron if you're using it for the first time.

1½ cups all-purpose flour
1½ teaspoons baking powder
1 tablespoon plus 1 teaspoon sugar
½ teaspoon salt
2 tablespoons wheat germ (an option that will change
   the flavor a bit—Bill loves it!)
2 large eggs
1¼ cups whole or 2% milk
6 tablespoons melted butter (not clarified, reserve
   1 tablespoon to brush on waffle iron)

Preheat the waffle iron (check the manufacturer's setting and adjust according to how well done you like your waffles). Using a fork, cut the dry ingredients together thoroughly in a large bowl (6-quart is ideal). Beat the eggs and milk together using your fork or a whisk and pour into the dry ingredients. Mix together with the fork until there are no large lumps, but as with pancakes, don't overmix! Cut in 5 tablespoons of the butter last.

When the iron is ready, brush some butter on the top and bottom of the iron and ladle (or spoon—whatever you use) on enough batter (about 3 tablespoons) so that the batter will not squirt out the edges when you close the iron. This waffle won't come out a perfect square and you'll make a mess if you try it. The waffle iron will probably beep or blink a light to tell you when your waffle is done. Serve with Orange Butter (see following recipe) and maple syrup.

Note: The best way to reheat waffles is in a toaster, provided you have one large enough to accommodate them. Microwaving makes them tough. In the oven they will dry out, or if you wrap them in foil, they'll steam and get limp.

Orange Butter

1 pound unsalted, sweetened butter
Zest and juice of 1 orange

While the butter is beating in the food processor, grate the outside of the orange to get a fine zest (avoid any of the white part under the outside rind). Juice the orange. The butter will turn white when it is properly whipped. At this point you can easily blend in the zest and juice. Voilà! Orange butter. Store it in the refrigerator as you would regular butter.

Pecan Waffles

Makes 10 waffles

These waffles have been on Good Enough to Eat's breakfast menu since we opened twenty years ago. I tried taking them (along with the Orange Butter) off around five years ago because, well, because there's only just so many things you can have on a menu, and I wanted to try something new. I nearly had a full-scale riot on my hands and had to run into the prep room to toast some pecans and whip up a batch of Orange Butter. If it ain't broke . . .

Good Enough to Eat Waffle batter (p. 53)
¾ cup shelled pecan halves
1 tablespoon melted butter for the iron
¾ cup coarsely chopped pecans

Preheat the oven to 350 degrees and prepare the batter.

Distribute the ¾ cup of pecan halves over the surface of a dry cookie sheet and toast in the oven for 7 to 10 minutes, turning them after 5 minutes. (This timing should work if your oven is accurately calibrated. Use an oven thermometer to check—this is important for all your baking.) Watch the nuts. If they are undercooked they can be a bit soggy; if they get burned, they will be bitter. You'll get to know the wonderful nutty aroma that signals they're done.

Once the toasting is done and the pecans are safely out of the oven, you can begin to cook waffles.

Preheat the waffle iron—you could do this during the last minute of the toasting. Brush melted butter over the top and bottom waffle iron grids. When the waffle iron tells you it's ready, ladle in enough batter to fill the grid and begin to reach the outside edges. Immediately follow the batter with a rounded tablespoon of the chopped pecans evenly scattered over the surface of the batter. Close the iron.

When the waffle iron tells you it's time, remove the waffle by picking up a corner with a fork and pulling it out. Waffles are best when served right away. You could try to keep them warm in the oven, but they'll get limp. At home, if I'm facing a backup, I pile them on a plate warmed over the stove pilot light.

Each waffle you make should follow the same sequence outlined above. Serve with maple syrup and some toasted pecans scattered on top.

Strawberry-Almond Waffles

Makes 10 waffles

These waffles take the place of the Pecan Waffles on our summer menu, and if you remember Dave, they're his daughter, Isabel's, favorite.

Good Enough to Eat Waffle batter (p. 53)
1 cup blanched sliced almonds
1 tablespoon melted butter for iron
10 to 12 large ripe strawberries, sliced lengthwise about
⅛ inch thick

Preheat the oven to 350 degrees and make the batter.

Distribute ½ cup of the almonds over a dry cookie sheet and toast in the oven for about 5 minutes, tossing them in between. Remove from the oven when they get golden brown.

Preheat the waffle iron, and when it tells you it's ready, brush some butter over the grids. Making sure you've still got the iron's "go" signal, spoon on about 3 tablespoons of batter and distribute a level (or slightly shallow) tablespoon of the untoasted almonds over the surface. Close the iron. Take note that the strawberries are *not* cooked into the waffles!

When the iron tells you the waffle is done, pull the waffle out and serve with equal amounts of toasted almonds and sliced strawberries on top. Don't forget the maple syrup!

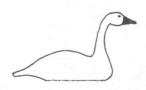

Lemon–Poppy Seed Waffles

Makes 10 waffles

*T*hese go on the restaurant's summer brunch menu as a special. They've become enormously popular since I introduced them two years ago.

Good Enough to Eat Waffle batter (p. 53)
Zest of 1 lemon (see p. 54 for zesting)
1 tablespoon melted butter for iron
2 tablespoons poppy seeds

During the preparation of the waffle batter, add the lemon zest to the milk mixture (less chance of clumping here) before adding the liquids to the dry ingredients and mixing.

Preheat the waffle iron.

Brush melted butter over the grids. When the iron tells you it's ready, spoon about 3 tablespoons of batter onto the lower grid. Sprinkle a dusting of poppy seeds over the surface of the batter and close the iron. When the waffle iron beeps or blinks or otherwise gives you the signal, take your waffle out.

This waffle is great with Maple Whipped Cream (p. 124) and some sliced peaches.

Belgian Waffles

Makes 10 waffles

This reminds me so strongly of my childhood in Belgium: sitting on the boardwalk at the seaside in the north, eating a waffle topped with crème fraîche, crème Chantilly (a lighter version of our whipped cream), or just some powdered sugar.

You could get the Belgian waffles anytime, day or night. At teatime, called quatre heure *in Belgium, we all could have a waffle, topped with a scoop of vanilla ice cream, and a cup of coffee (kids, too!).*

Note: *The true Belgian waffle is made with yeast, but it is time-consuming to make. My Americanized recipe is quicker and easier and comes very close to the texture and taste of the original.*

1½ **cups all-purpose white flour**
½ **teaspoon salt**
1½ **teaspoons baking powder**
2 **teaspoons plus 2 tablespoons sugar**
1½ **cups milk**
½ **teaspoon pure vanilla extract**
3 **eggs (separated)**
6 **tablespoons melted butter plus 1 tablespoon for the iron**

Combine the flour, salt, baking powder, and the 2 teaspoons of sugar in a large bowl and mix thoroughly. Combine the milk, vanilla, and 2 of the egg yolks in a separate bowl and lightly beat them together. (Sorry about that extra egg yolk!) Now pour the yolky milk mixture into the dry ingredients and stir them together with a fork. That done, cut in the 6 tablespoons of melted butter.

Preheat the waffle iron.

In yet a third bowl—clean and dry—whisk together the 3 egg whites and the 2 tablespoons of sugar until they begin to hold a soft peak. Now, take a big tablespoonful of the egg whites and mix it through the batter with a fork. Once that's done, turn out all of the beaten egg whites onto the batter with a rubber spatula. Using your spatula, fold the egg whites into the batter, cutting a figure eight, toward and away from you, putting the "8" on its side. Rotate the bowl a couple of times during the folding to incorporate the whites into the batter. You want to mix the whites into the batter, but over-mixing will knock air out of the egg whites, and you don't want too much of that.

Now proceed to cook the Belgian waffles as you would any other waffle. Serve them with some berries such as strawberries or raspberries (Belgium didn't have blueberries), Mock Crème Fraîche (p. 189), and a few shakes of confectioners' sugar. They're sweet enough, so you won't need maple syrup.

Norwegian Waffles

Makes 10 waffles

This recipe came to me by way of my maple syrup supplier in Canada, who is of Norwegian descent. Norwegian waffles are traditionally served with jam and not maple syrup!

1 cup all-purpose white flour
2 teaspoons baking powder
1 teaspoon baking soda
1½ teaspoons ground cardamom
¼ teaspoon salt
3 eggs, separated
⅓ cup sugar
2 cups sour cream
1 Granny Smith apple, grated
3 tablespoons melted butter plus 1 tablespoon for the iron

Preheat the waffle iron. (In Norway these waffles are made with the Belgian waffle iron with its deep peaks and valleys. Many American-made irons have adopted this design; however, I don't think it matters that much to the waffle.)

In a large bowl, combine the flour, baking powder, baking soda, cardamom, and salt. In a separate bowl, whisk the 3 egg yolks, then add the sugar, sour cream, and grated apple and whisk together. Now combine the yolk mixture and the dry ingredients and blend them thoroughly. Drizzle the 3 tablespoons of melted butter into the batter and cut it in with a fork.

Using a clean, dry whisk and bowl, whip the egg whites to soft peaks. Now swirl a tablespoon of the egg whites through the batter—this facilitates the folding in of the rest of the egg whites. With your rubber spatula fold in the egg whites using a figure-eight motion—the motion puts the "8" on its side—toward and then away from you; turn the bowl a couple of times, completing the blending.

Brush some melted butter onto the grids of your iron, and when the iron tells you it's ready, spoon in some batter. Cook the waffles as you would any others, following the signals of the waffle iron. The waffles should be golden brown when done.

In Norway these waffles are served with lingonberry jam, which is carried by some gourmet food shops. Try them with Strawberry Jam (p. 154) or Cranberry Preserves (p. 156).

FRENCH TOAST

I went to college in Aix-en-Provence and spent quite a lot of time in Paris, and I can say for a fact that I have never seen French toast on any menu in a French restaurant. What we call French toast the French call *pain perdu*, which translates to "lost bread" in English. It is very well known in the kitchens of every French household.

Bread dipped in egg custard, fried in butter, and eaten with a little powdered sugar on top was a way of utilizing stale French bread. That wonderful bread that is ubiquitous on every French table is nothing more than flour, yeast, water, and salt. It is delicious when fresh but goes stale within a day. The moisture lost in going stale is restored by the custard.

I'm not sure what keeps store-bought bread from going stale . . . *hmmm?* At the restaurant we slice our homemade Cinnamon-Swirl and Pumpkin Breads early in the morning so that they lose some of their moisture. That way they won't fall apart when dipped in the egg and milk. If you happen to have "lost" any bread around the house, find it again with the following recipes!

Fundamental French Toast

Makes 8 slices

4 eggs
½ cup buttermilk or whole milk
¼ teaspoon cinnamon
1 teaspoon pure vanilla extract
Pinch salt
Pinch black pepper
8 slices white bread (should be good quality—"lost"
   or otherwise)
Butter for the pan or griddle

Preheat the griddle or frying pan. Whisk together the eggs, buttermilk, cinnamon, vanilla, salt, and pepper in a glass pie pan. We'll call this the custard. Dip each slice of bread into the custard, coating each side, and then arrange the slices in a pyramid on a plate. If the bread is very fresh (soft), don't soak the slices too long or they will fall apart when you pick them up.

Butter the griddle and lay on the slices. If you're using a frying pan, make sure the butter is hot before putting in the bread. As butter heats it loses its opacity (clarifies). You don't want the butter to smoke or burn. If this is a worry, you can drizzle a little bit of vegetable oil into the butter. The butter will still burn, but not as quickly. Cook the toast to a rich brown—lift a corner with your spatula to check—and turn. Continue to cook until done. You can test for doneness by patting the toast lightly with a finger. As the toast cooks it will start to feel denser to the touch. If your griddle or pan is superhot, you can sear the surface of the toast and the inside will be mushy. If the heat is too low, the toast will take too long to cook and will get dry. Play with the heat and touch to get your toast perfect. If you use a frying pan, shake it in a forward-backward motion to make sure the toast doesn't stick. Serve immediately with maple syrup.

In the summer we serve our French toast with slices of fresh peaches.

Pumpkin Bread French Toast with Pear-Cranberry Topping

Makes 8 slices

This is a dish for breakfast in the fall—the kids are back in school, the sweaters are out of the mothballs, and the maple trees are dressed in red, yellow, and orange.

Follow the recipe for Fundamental French Toast (p. 61) using Pumpkin Bread (see recipe on p. 101) instead of white bread. Cut 8 slices and let them dry out a few hours if you can, so that they will hold up in the custard. Pumpkin Bread is denser and will need a little more time absorbing the French toast custard. It is richer than the Fundamental French Toast, so perhaps you won't want to eat as much! Well . . . your tummy will tell!

Pear-Cranberry Topping

Makes 2 cups

1 teaspoon powdered ginger
Pinch salt
Pinch black pepper
⅓ cup cranberry juice
3 tablespoons orange juice (squeeze ½ orange)
5 tablespoons dark brown sugar
½ teaspoon vanilla extract
1 teaspoon finely grated fresh ginger root (or use another
    ½ teaspoon powdered)
3 hard Bartlett pears—peeled, cored, cubed (8 pieces per
    pear)
½ cup cranberries

In a heavy-bottomed 2-quart saucepan over high heat, toast the dry ginger, salt, and pepper until a beautiful aroma fills your kitchen (about 7 minutes). You are making "magic." Turn off the heat and let the "magic" cool for a minute so that you won't get spattered when you add the liquids.

Now carefully add the juices, as well as the shell of the juiced orange, the brown sugar, vanilla, and fresh ginger, if using it. Cook over a low heat for about 10 minutes, until the sugar is dissolved, stirring with a long-handled wooden spoon. Bring to a boil, add the pears and cranberries, and stir to coat the fruit.

After the mixture returns to a boil, reduce to a simmer. Cook about 15 minutes longer—the fruit should be cooked but still retain its shape. Remove the fruit from the juice using a slotted spoon and reserve (you can leave the orange shell in the juice). Continue to cook the juice for another 10 to 15 minutes, until it becomes a syrup. Remove from the heat and discard the orange shell.

You can now recombine the fruit and syrup and serve as a

topping on the Pumpkin Bread French Toast. Be judicious with the maple syrup, as this topping is sweet.

This is also an excellent topping for roast pork loin!

Nota bene: I would like to add a caution here about all mixtures that incorporate heated sugar: When at their highest temperature—during cooking or just off the heat— they can cause severe burns. When stirring or pouring, always use an oven mitt or dish towel; let such mixtures cool 10 minutes or so before tasting—and *be careful!*

Cinnamon-Swirl French Toast with Autumn Marmalade Topping

Makes 8 slices

The French toast on the menu at Good Enough to Eat is made with our own Cinnamon-Swirl Bread (see recipe on p. 88). In the summer we serve Cinnamon-Swirl French Toast with sliced fresh peaches, but strawberries, blueberries, or any fresh seasonal berry or fruit can be used. My husband, Bill, likes the canned apricot halves. The Autumn Marmalade Topping is great served with this French toast during the cooler months of fall and winter.

Follow the recipe for Fundamental French Toast on p. 61, using 8 slices of Cinnamon-Swirl Bread that you've allowed to get a little "lost."

Autumn Marmalade Topping

Makes about 2 cups

1 cup water
⅓ cup dried apricots (slice each apricot in half)
⅓ cup dried blueberries
⅓ cup dried cherries or cranberries
1 English Breakfast tea bag

Pinch salt
¼ cup orange marmalade

Bring the water to a boil in a 2-quart pot and turn off the
heat. Add the dried fruit, tea bag, and salt, and steep for 15
minutes. Remove the tea bag. Stir in the marmalade with a
long wooden spoon and bring to a boil again, then reduce the
heat and simmer for 15 to 20 minutes or until the liquid
becomes a syrup. Take it off the heat and let it cool while you
cook the French toast.

The Autumn Marmalade Topping will still be nice and
warm when you're ready to spoon it on your Cinnamon-Swirl
French Toast. It's sweet, so you may want to go easy on the
maple syrup.

Monte Cristo

Makes 4 sandwiches

*There's something about diners that I approve of—good food at
reasonable prices, served quickly in sizable quantities with a
minimum of ceremony and froufrou. About a year ago I was in
my Long Island City neighborhood diner, and I noticed
someone pouring maple syrup over what looked to me like a
grilled-cheese sandwich. Hugo, my waiter, told me that it was a
Monte Cristo—ham and Swiss cheese between two slices of
French toast. Inspiration struck, and I devised my own Monte
Cristo as a Good Enough to Eat brunch special. Here's the
recipe.*

8 slices Fundamental French Toast
20 ounces Glazed Baked Ham (p. 175) sliced for 4
    sandwiches
12 ounces Brie sliced for 4 sandwiches
2 tablespoons butter and ½ teaspoon vegetable oil
    melted together

Prepare the Fundamental French Toast according to the recipe instructions on p. 61.

Arrange the ham and Brie (Brie on top) on the 4 slices of French toast that will be the bottoms of your sandwiches. Place them under the broiler long enough to melt the cheese. Remove from the broiler and put the remaining 4 slices of French toast on top.

Using a medium heat—the griddle will probably still be hot from the French toast, and a frying pan heats quickly—cook the sandwiches for about 2 minutes on each side. This is additional cooking time for the French toast, so you may want to undercook when you first prepare it.

At the restaurant we serve the Monte Cristo with seasonal fruit on the side. The acidity of the fruit makes a nice balance for the heavier flavors of the sandwich. Top with maple syrup.

Challah Hole-in-the-Bread with Grand Marnier Bananas

Makes 8 slices

My father and mother retired to a picturesque town in Connecticut after twenty-eight years of life in Brussels, Belgium. They do all sorts of volunteer work in the community. In one such effort, my dad, along with many other volunteers, teaches an English-as-second-language class to adults who have immigrated to the area. To thank the volunteers, the students cook a specialty meal for them—usually something ethnic in character. The following recipe was derived from a dish cooked by a woman with a thick Italian accent and was described to Dad as Challah (with the ch pronounced as in cheese) French Toast with bananas. After he figured out the pronunciation, Dad passed the recipe on to me. The Grand Marnier is my embellishment.

8 slices of day-old Challah (see recipe p. 95), ½ inch
  thick
French toast custard (see p. 61)
1 tablespoon butter
1 teaspoon dark brown sugar
4 medium-firm bananas sliced into ¼-inch disks
2 tablespoons Grand Marnier

Preheat the oven to 300 degrees and the griddle to medium-high. Cut a 2½-inch hole in each slice of bread using a biscuit or cookie cutter or the point of a sharp paring knife. Having prepared the custard in a flat-bottomed glass pie pan according to the Fundamental French Toast recipe, dip the Challah slices in the custard and stack them on a plate. Save the leftover custard for the bananas.

Combine the butter and brown sugar and cook in a heavy frying pan over a medium-high heat for about 1 minute or until it bubbles, stirring constantly. It will start to caramelize, at which point you add the bananas. Sauté the bananas for about 30 seconds on each side, until they are coated with the caramel glaze. Pour in the Grand Marnier. It may flame up, so be careful. It will take about 15 seconds for the alcohol to burn off. Remove from the heat and put the bananas into the leftover custard.

Now proceed to cook the custard-soaked Challah on the buttered griddle or frying pan (not the same one you used for the glaze) 3 minutes on the first side. Turn and cook for 1 minute, then spoon the bananas and custard into the hole. Cook for 1 minute to sear the bottom; turn and cook for 1 more minute, locking the banana-custard mixture in the hole. Remove from the heat.

Place the Challah Hole-in-the-Breads in a glass baking pan and bake in the 300-degree oven for 10 minutes. The baking finishes the cooking and allows the flavors to mingle. Serve with a sprinkle of powdered sugar and strawberries cut in half. Have the maple syrup on the table, and leave the caps with their little green leaves on the strawberries—they're pretty!

Matzo Brei

Makes 2 four-and-one-half-inch servings

Our good friend Norman tells how, when he was a starving actor living on the Lower East Side of Manhattan, he used to collect chowder crackers and saltines from restaurants to make his own matzo brei. It should work, but I've never tried it. Norman is no longer starving, and I don't believe he is still collecting crackers—but with Norman you never know. Anyway, here's a conventional recipe that's on the Good Enough to Eat menu for the week of Passover.

2 eggs
¼ cup milk
½ teaspoon sugar
1 teaspoon vanilla extract
¼ teaspoon cinnamon
Pinch salt
Pinch black pepper
2½ matzos broken into pieces
½ cup boiling water
1 tablespoon butter (for the pan)

Beat the eggs, milk, sugar, vanilla, cinnamon, salt, and pepper together in a large bowl. Put the matzos in a colander over the sink and pour the boiling water over them, letting them drain immediately. Press the softened matzos into the egg mixture to saturate.

Heat approximately 1½ teaspoons of the butter in a number 10 frying pan until hot (bubbling) but not burning (turning brown). Put half of the matzo mixture into the center of the pan, and with the edge of your spatula, press it down to form a pancake. Cook about 3 minutes on each side, and plate for serving. Heat some more butter in the pan and repeat for the second matzo.

Traditionally, matzo brei is served with sour cream, jam, or applesauce. No maple syrup this time!

Note: Matzo brei takes the place of French Toast over Passover because matzo is unleavened (not made with yeast).

FIVE

Cereals

Growing up in Belgium, I don't remember ever eating cereals for breakfast. I'm sure they must have existed. Maybe my parents had a prejudice against them and never bought them. Of course, coming to the States in the summers, I would see stacks and stacks of cereals in supermarket aisles, with cartoon characters and sports stars beckoning from brightly colored boxes.

However, I don't serve any cereals at my restaurant that come in boxes except for the oatmeal, which is packaged that way. The few cereals I offer here are, I believe, quite unusual and unlike anything you've probably had before. Like many of my recipes, I came up with them partly by chance and partly through experimentation.

Swiss Breakfast (Muesli)

Makes 2 to 3 servings

*B*ill, my husband, called this cereal Swiss Breakfast when he made it for me. He said it came from a recipe in a book by Gaylord Hauser. Hauser was in the vanguard of health food enthusiasts. His books are now out of print, unfortunately, so I can't say whether this is Mr. Hauser's recipe or Bill's version of it. Knowing my husband, I would bet on the latter.

Bill claimed that this cereal gave him a jolt of energy and, along with his pancakes, was a breakfast staple when he was on the road, acting in various parts of the country.

½ cup rolled oats
½ cup wheat germ
2 tablespoons dark raisins
½ cup slivered almonds
2 Granny Smith apples
Juice of ½ lemon
3 tablespoons honey (more or less to taste)
1 banana, sliced (optional)
Milk for serving

On the evening before concocting this cereal, put the oats and wheat germ in a glass container and add just enough water to saturate. Cover and refrigerate until morning. (The theory is that the grains begin to germinate, rendering them more digestible and their vitamin content—lots of Bs—more accessible.)

In the morning, put the grains in a large bowl and add the raisins and almonds. Toss them together with a fork and tablespoon (like a salad). Shred the Grannies with their peels on and squeeze the ½ lemon over the shredded apple. (Lemon juice keeps the apple from turning brown, and adds tang.)

Add the shredded apple to the grain mixture and toss together. Drizzle on the honey, or leave the honey to be added individually with the banana and milk.

Let me know if you get a "jolt" later that morning.

Note: Considering the prices of boxed cereals these days, this is quite economical to make.

Granola

Makes 8 to 10 servings

Transplanted New Yorkers who are devotees of our granola write to me (and phone) begging me to mail it to them. I have done so on occasions when it seemed to be a matter of life and death. However, I'm not really set up for that sort of thing—practically or emotionally—so don't get any ideas!

This recipe has evolved, but it was originally given to me by one of my first employees. Her name was Hanna and she was just out of college. She said her granola was an "old family recipe," as so many great recipes are. I don't know what became of Hanna, but I sure would like to thank her again for getting me started on this granola.

Vegetable oil spray
5 cups rolled oats
¼ cup wheat germ
½ cup mixed halved walnuts, pecans, and almonds
1½ cups sweetened shredded coconut
½ cup sesame seeds
¼ cup sunflower seeds
1¾ tablespoons cinnamon
¼ teaspoon nutmeg
½ teaspoon kosher salt
½ cup honey
¾ cup (1 stick plus 2 tablespoons) butter, melted
¾ cup prunes (pitted, sliced)
¾ cup dried apricots (sliced)
½ cup dried cranberries

Preheat the oven to 350 degrees. Lightly spray 2 baking sheets (12 x 18 inches) with vegetable oil.

In your largest bowl combine all the dry ingredients (grains, nuts, coconut, seeds, spices) with your hands (clean hands!). Drizzle in the honey and work the melted butter through the cereal with a spoon. Spread the mixture over the baking sheets, pressing lightly until it is ½ inch thick.

Bake for 15 minutes. It should get crisp and deep chestnut brown, but watch it—don't let it burn. When it looks ready, take it out and break the granola into large pieces. Turn them over and bake for another 5 minutes.

Take the granola out of the oven and break it up into small chunks in your large bowl. Add the prunes, apricots, and cranberries to the cereal after it has cooled completely. Serve with cold milk or yogurt. In the winter we serve our granola with sliced bananas, in the summer, with fresh blueberries and strawberries.

Note: This granola can be stored in brown paper bags in the bread box or other dry place for up to 5 days. Do not include the dried fruit with granola you are storing. Do not refrigerate!

Savory Cereal

Makes 4 two-cup servings

*H*ere's a hot cereal from the land of the mystics, some of whom claim that it will cure asthma, congestion, indigestion, bronchitis, and skin irritations. I don't know about that, but it makes a wonderful, exotic breakfast with a hot cup of Chai (p. 198) on a winter morning.

Note: *You'll have to find an Indian market for many of the ingredients.*

8 cups water
1 cup millet
1 teaspoon fenugreek seeds
1 teaspoon cumin seeds
1 teaspoon coram
¼ cup shredded coconut
¼ cup finely chopped or grated onion
1 tablespoon finely chopped serrano chile, with seeds
½ cup rolled oats
4 dates, pitted and finely chopped
1½ cups seeded, finely chopped tomato
2 tablespoons peeled and minced ginger
1½ teaspoons kosher salt
2 tablespoons finely chopped cilantro

Bring the water to a boil in a large (8-quart) pot. Add the millet, fenugreek, cumin, and coram. After the water comes back to a boil, reduce the heat and simmer for 30 minutes, stirring occasionally with a wooden spoon.

Add the remaining ingredients except the cilantro and simmer for 15 minutes, stirring occasionally. Turn off the heat and stir in the cilantro. Let sit for another 3 minutes, and serve. Savory cereal is not eaten with sugar or milk. *Om!*

Oatmeal

Serves 4

Wasn't it oatmeal that Oliver wanted "more" of in Oliver Twist? It was probably called gruel back then. Oatmeal has never needed to be sophisticated to be appreciated. It's very basic. Despite its common pedigree, we have developed a following of oatmeal connoisseurs who hold us to a high standard. It is perennially popular, particularly in the cooler months, and epitomizes so well the advice we heard as children: "Start each day with a good breakfast!"

Note: I don't care for the instant oatmeals. Quaker rolled oats is fine. McCain's Irish is a little crunchy and is the one I use at Good Enough.

1¼ cups rolled oats
2¼ cups water
½ teaspoon salt
2 tablespoons dark raisins

Put everything into a pot and cover. Bring to a boil, then lower the heat and cook for 5 minutes or so. Stir frequently if you like creamy oatmeal. Oatmeal thickens quickly, so be careful not to burn it at the bottom of the pot.

Serve with cream, brown sugar, and a buttered slice of toasted Cinnamon-Swirl Bread.

Note: My husband, Bill, puts a tablespoon of wheat germ on his oatmeal. The toasted, nutty flavor of the wheat germ complements oatmeal very well. A bowl of hot oatmeal with brown sugar, cream, and wheat germ was his German grandmother's version of chicken soup—it "cures what ails ya"!

SIX

Breads

I have divided this chapter into two sections: "Quick Breads" and "Yeast Breads." They are significantly different from each other. Quick breads are batter breads and their preparation is similar to that used for muffins, particularly the business of how you combine the ingredients. I will constantly harp on the nuances of composition out of the conviction that it is the technique of preparation that makes the difference between great food and the merely edible.

Like all living things, yeast is rife with idiosyncrasies, as are doughs made with it. I'll have lots to say about that subject in the section on yeast breads. We will continue our acquaintance with yeast in the recipes for Good Enough to Eat Biscuits and English Muffins.

Some general admonitions:

- Make sure your oven is correctly calibrated. Have an oven thermometer on hand to check and adjust if necessary.
- As a general rule, it is better to underwork rather than overwork doughs and batters. Overworking (too much mixing, blending, beating, kneading, and so on) will produce tough bread.
- Don't forget the salt! I have found this to be the most frequently forgotten ingredient.

I once read an article that contended that if you're trying to sell your house, bake some bread just before the prospective buyer arrives. The aroma is mesmeric and can be of great assistance in getting your asking price!

QUICK BREADS

Cornbread

Makes 9 servings

It's funny, but I can always tell which of my bakers (or cooks) has made the cornbread on any particular day. They all use the same recipe—this one—but cornbread seems to absorb person- alities. Try it, and learn something about yourself! This batter can make either pan bread or muffins.

1 tablespoon bacon fat, melted in baking pan (or butter or
    vegetable shortening)
1½ cups all-purpose flour
1½ cups coarsely ground yellow cornmeal
¼ cup sugar
2 teaspoons baking powder
½ teaspoon baking soda
½ teaspoon salt
1 egg
1½ cups buttermilk
8 ounces (½ cup, 1 stick) butter, melted
1 cup corn kernels (I like the canned corn best—drain
    the water off)
Cornmeal for dusting the pan

Preheat the oven to 350 degrees. Heat the bacon fat in a 9 x 9-inch Pyrex baking pan in the oven. (If you are making muffins, put liners into the cups and grease the top of the muffin pan with some butter to keep the domes from sticking.)

In a large bowl, combine the flour, cornmeal, sugar, baking powder, baking soda, and salt. Mix well, ensuring that there are no lumps of baking powder. (Overmixing only becomes a danger after the liquid and dry ingredients are combined.)

In another bowl, whisk the egg and the buttermilk together to a smooth yellow color. Pour this egg mixture into the dry ingredients, stirring with a wooden spoon to combine. Next, drizzle in the melted butter, stirring it in with the spoon. You want to thread the butter through the batter, so don't overstir. Finally, add the corn kernels, again stirring to combine.

Pull the oven rack out of the heated oven and be sure the melted bacon fat is evenly distributed over the bottom and sides of the pan. Pour the batter into the center of the pan, using your fingers or a rubber spatula to get the remainder out of the bowl.

Bake the bread 30 to 40 minutes. (For muffins, bake 20 to 25 minutes.) Turn the pan once halfway through cooking. Check for doneness close to the end of the cooking time by sticking the bread with a fork. If the tines come out dry to the touch, the bread is done.

Let the cornbread cool for 10 minutes before slicing. It's great warm with some honey. At the restaurant, we heat cornbread (both sides of a slice) on a buttered griddle for a dinner appetizer. It is phenomenally popular.

Banana Bread

Makes 1 loaf (8 to 10 slices)

This is a favorite for afternoon teas with other neighborhood mothers—on Saturdays, that is, after soccer. Along with the cornbread, it is also the favorite of my sons when they have to bring a snack to school for their class to share.

6 tablespoons butter plus extra for the pan (soft)
½ cup sugar
1½ cups all-purpose flour
¼ cup wheat germ or whole-wheat flour
½ teaspoon salt
2 teaspoons baking powder
¼ teaspoon baking soda
3 medium-sized bananas (2 should be very ripe—soft, with skins blackening)
¼ cup buttermilk or whole yogurt
Zest of one lemon
2 eggs
½ cup coarsely chopped walnuts (optional)

Preheat the oven to 350 degrees.

Grease a 1-pound loaf pan (8½ x 4½ inches) with some butter, then dust it with flour. (To flour the pan, put a scant tablespoon of flour in, shake the flour around, rotating the pan until it is coated, and then knock out any excess flour.)

In a standing mixer (paddle attachment) or food processor, cream the butter and sugar together until the mixture is white. While this is going on, you can combine the dry ingredients—flour, wheat germ, salt, baking powder, and baking soda—in a large bowl. Once the butter-sugar mixture is white, turn off the mixer.

In a separate container mash the 2 ripe bananas together with the buttermilk and lemon zest. Beat the eggs in your measuring cup, then blend with the butter-sugar mixture at low speed. Stop the mixer and push down whatever accumulates on the sides of the mixer bowl with a rubber spatula.

Add the banana mash, blend, then stop the mixer and push down the mixture on the sides. Now add the dry ingredients and combine at low speed. Do this last step as quickly as possible, stopping the mixer to push batter down from the sides. Run the mixer one more time to ensure thorough mixing, but do not overmix.

Slice the remaining yellow banana into ⅛-inch disks, and add it and the walnuts (if using) to the mixer. Run the mixer, just long enough to combine. Run the spatula around the mixer bowl to check for pockets of dry mix that weren't blended.

Use a rubber spatula to transfer the batter to the prepared baking pan and bake for about 40 minutes, or until a fork comes out dry and clean.

Let the Banana Bread cool in its pan for 15 minutes before slicing to serve.

Nondairy Banana Bread

Makes 1 loaf (8 to 10 slices)

About a year ago my husband, Bill, and I found out that our youngest son, Conner, was allergic to dairy products—he can't digest them. I developed this recipe because Banana Bread is very popular in our household. When Bill was running marathons, he found out that bananas were an excellent source of the minerals that get depleted through sweating. He eats wheat germ as a source of B vitamins, since he seems to be allergic to the synthesized Bs.

Also, my kids don't like nuts, and Bill and I do, so . . . here's what I came up with.

½ to ⅔ cup dark brown sugar
⅓ cup applesauce
2 bananas (1 very ripe; 1 yellow and sliced into ⅛-inch
   rounds)
2 eggs
1½ cups all-purpose flour (or ¾ cup, plus ¾ cup
   whole-wheat flour)
¼ cup wheat germ
2½ teaspoons baking powder
½ teaspoon salt
¼ teaspoon cinnamon
¼ cup walnut pieces

Preheat the oven to 350 degrees. Grease a 1-pound loaf pan
(8½ x 4½ inches) with some vegetable shortening.

In the standing mixer (using the paddle attachment) or
food processor, cream the brown sugar and applesauce. Mash
the ripe banana in a separate container. Beat the eggs in a
measuring cup.

Combine the flour, wheat germ, baking powder, salt, and
cinnamon in a large bowl.

Add the beaten eggs to the mixer bowl and combine them
with the applesauce-sugar mixture at low speed (pulse on the
processor). Stop the mixer and push down whatever has
climbed the sides of the bowl with a spatula. Add the banana
mash and mix to combine. Again, stop the mixer and push
down the side stuff with a spatula.

Now put the dry ingredients and mix at low speed to combine. Stop the mixer and push down the batter on the sides.
Then push the spatula all around the bottom of the bowl to
check for vagrant pockets of dry mix. If there are none, fine;
if there are, break them up with the spatula and then turn on
the mixer for a couple more seconds.

Finally, add the banana rounds and run the mixer a bit to
combine.

Spatula the batter into your greased loaf pan. Now scatter
some walnuts over half of the loaf and punch them down
with the handle of the spoon. Add the rest of the nuts and

tap to various depths, trying to disperse them evenly. If you have a dough cutter or something clean and nonreactive (plastic, wood, stainless steel) to put in as a divider, it makes this easier, but you have to take it out before baking. Bake for about 50 minutes. Check for doneness after 40 minutes. When the fork comes out clean and dry, it's done.

Zucchini-Prune Bread

Makes 1 loaf (8 to 10 slices)

The kids on our block who come over to play with my boys love this bread, and a few of them have asked what was in it. I'd never tell. Can you imagine the reaction if I told them it was squash and prunes?

Z-P Bread is spicy, filling, and nutritious. You can easily substitute grated carrots for the zucchini and golden raisins for the prunes. I'd leave the sunflower seeds in.

¾ cup (about 12 ounces) grated young zucchini
⅓ cup prunes, pitted and slivered
⅓ cup raw sunflower seeds
¾ cup plus 1 tablespoon all-purpose flour plus additional flour for dusting pan
¾ cup plus 1 tablespoon whole-wheat flour
1½ teaspoons cinnamon
½ teaspoon nutmeg
⅛ teaspoon cloves
½ teaspoon salt
1 teaspoon baking soda
1 cup sugar
6 tablespoons (¾ stick) butter (soft)
⅓ cup vegetable oil
2 eggs
1 teaspoon pure vanilla extract

Brush your 1-pound loaf pan (8½ x 4½ inches) with some butter (or vegetable shortening), and flour the inside, shaking out the excess. Preheat the oven to 325 degrees.

Wash the zucchini well and do not peel them. On the larger holes, grate the zucchini down to the cores, which you discard. Combine the zucchini with the prune slivers and sunflower seeds in a bowl.

In a large bowl combine the dry ingredients: flours, cinnamon, nutmeg, cloves, salt, and baking soda.

Cream the sugar with the butter in the food processor until white, then gradually add the vegetable oil. Turn off the processor and scrape down with a rubber spatula anything that has accumulated on the inside of the processor. (Do this after each time you run the processor.)

Beat the eggs with the vanilla and add to the processor and beat in.

Add the dry ingredients and process just long enough to blend. Stop the processor, scrape down the sides, and run the spatula down and around the processor, searching for any pockets of unblended dry ingredients. If you find any, break them up and process a few seconds more.

Now add the prunes, zucchini, and seeds and process to incorporate them through the batter. Use the spatula to transfer the batter to the prepared baking pan and bake in the oven for 50 minutes. Check with a fork for doneness after about 40 minutes. When the fork comes out clean and dry, you'll know it's done.

Let the bread cool in the pan for 15 minutes before removing or slicing it. Zucchini-Prune Bread will store in the refrigerator for 3 to 4 days, but it will start to sweat and get sticky. It's best to eat it up in a couple of days. (I've never had one last longer in my house.) Heat a slice on both sides on the griddle and serve it with some cream cheese.

YEAST BREADS

It was when I became a mother that I discovered the proper metaphor for baking yeast breads: babies! They both cry out for attention and tender loving care. They both are capable of surprising and humbling you. They dislike cold drafts. They are not amenable to instruction, good intentions, or wishful thinking, but are rather osmotically reactive to their immediate environment. When they are happy and healthy, however, they can fill you with bliss and the sense that God is smiling on you. A perfect bread dough is like a baby's bottom: smooth and silky, not too moist and not too dry.

I have a neighbor living a few doors down from me who invited me to her house for a gathering of her fellow bread bakers one afternoon. They had each brought a French bread they had made for a comparison test. All of the breads were magnificent—particularly my friend Sarah's. I was entranced by how rhapsodically they carried on over the crunchiness of the crusts and the size of the air holes in the breads. Bread makers are a special breed of perfectionists, and they taught me that in baking my own bread for Good Enough to Eat, I faced a special kind of challenge.

Well, I do make all the bread I serve at the restaurant, so here goes. . . .

About Yeast

We use fresh yeast at the restaurant because we are baking every day. At home, however, I use dry yeast because it stores well, it is easier to use, and I have detected no discernible difference in the flavor or texture of the breads. Thus, all of these recipes call for dry yeast. If you do use fresh yeast: 1½ ounces of dry yeast equals 1¾ ounces fresh.

One packet of dry yeast contains 2½ teaspoons—a little less than a tablespoon—of yeast. This is adequate for one loaf of bread. As you become more practiced in bread making, you may want to vary the amount of yeast according to how yeasty you like the bread to taste. Remember that if you cut back on the yeast, it will take longer for the bread to rise!

When you mix the yeast with a little warm water and a pinch of sugar, use a ceramic or glass bowl. These materials dissipate heat less readily than metal. You want the water to be a constant 105 to 115 degrees in order for the "sponge" to grow successfully. You can check the temperature of the water as you would check the temperature of the milk warmed for a baby—if a drop on the wrist hurts, it's too hot. The sponge, as it is known in the baking trade, will take only 3 to 5 minutes to mature and should be incorporated into the dough immediately.

The "Chef"

Another term from the specialized lexicon of baking is the *chef*. It describes a portion of dough reserved from a day's baking to be incorporated into the next day's batch of dough. The mature dough seems to add a *je ne sais quoi* to the younger dough that enhances its flavor. A chef can be preserved in the refrigerator for only 48 hours before it becomes unusable (mold will get at it), so it is really only practical for those who are baking bread every day. The chef is the bread specialist's *sine qua non*, and those times when you've had an indescribably delicious piece of bread, it was undoubtably made using a chef.

A baker can sustain his (or her) chef by rotating and feeding it. There is an entertaining story about the relationship between a man and his chef in Anthony Bourdain's book *Kitchen Confidential*, in the chapter titled "Adam Real-Last-Name-Unknown." Bourdain's book resounds with truth as an under-the-apron view of the crazy world of professional cooks.

The Rest of It

I said that happy dough should look like a baby's bottom: silky and smooth. The moister the dough, the better; however, if it is too moist, it will be sticky and you won't be able to work with it. Only then should you add a dusting of flour. Don't automatically flour your board or rolling pin. If you get too much flour in your dough, it will produce dryer, tougher bread. If it is too dry, spritz some water on it.

Don't cook any food with strong flavors around rising dough—the dough will absorb them.

Dough rises best in a glass bowl at 65 to 75 degrees in a draft-free environment.

Dough should only rise to double its volume.

Knead with the heel of the hand, pushing into the center of the dough. You can rotate the dough, but don't fold it. The guiding principle is to knead sufficiently to incorporate all ingredients, *but* don't overknead. For some reason the less the dough is in contact with surfaces the better it is for the bread. When dough is evenly kneaded it becomes elastic—you can press into it with a thumb and it will bounce back.

You can make bread dough using a standing electric mixer with a dough hook or by hand. I like to work with my hands because I have learned to judge by feel how the dough is reacting to its environment—whether it's dry or humid—and whether I need to add a little flour or water to get the silky texture I'm looking (feeling) for.

Bake bread in the center of the oven to ensure proper circulation of heat. Burning can occur when pans are too low in the oven or too close to the sides. If the bread turns out too doughy in the center with a hard outside crust, the oven was too hot and the baking too rapid.

Now, if you're ready, let's bake some bread!

White Bread

Makes 1 loaf

*T*ake off any jewelry worn below the elbows—you are getting down to the basics with this bread.

⅓ cup whole milk
2 tablespoons soft butter plus more for greasing bowl
　　and pan
1 packet dry yeast
1 rounded tablespoon sugar plus a pinch for the sponge
¼ cup warm water (110 degrees)
2¼ cups flour (may need more for flouring)
½ teaspoon salt
2 eggs (1, along with 1 tablespoon milk, to be used
　　for glazing)

Heat the milk and 2 tablespoons of butter in a saucepan to scalding (when it bubbles at the edges), then remove from heat. Add the yeast and a pinch of sugar to the warm water. Stir with a plastic or wooden spoon. It should "sponge" in 3 to 5 minutes.

Using a standard mixer fitted with the dough hook, add the flour and salt to the mixer bowl and combine at very low speed. Whisk 1 egg in a bowl, then drizzle in a little of the milk and butter to temper it. Now combine all of the egg with the milk-butter mixture. Turn the mixer back on low and pour in the egg-milk-butter mixture. Let it beat together well. Stop the mixer and scrape down anything that has accumulated on the sides with a spatula.

Now add the sponge to the dough and mix it in until it disappears. Stop the mixer and scrape down whatever might have climbed the sides of the bowl.

Remove the dough to the board. If the dough seems sticky, check the bottom of the mixer bowl. There will probably be enough flour left there to lightly flour your board.

Knead the dough a couple of times, pushing the dough

with the heels of your hands into the center. Thumb check the dough: See if the dough bounces back from an impression made by the thumb. If it does, the dough is ready. If not, knead some more. The dough should be silky and smooth, like a baby's bottom!

Now put the dough into a ceramic or glass bowl that has been greased with butter. Roll the dough in the bowl until it is evenly coated with the butter. (The butter will keep it from getting crusty while rising.) Cover the bowl with a towel and place it in an area at 65 to 75 degrees, and free of drafts (or odors), to rise. It should double in size in about 1 hour.

Preheat the oven to 350 degrees. Grease the bread pan with some butter.

Remove the dough from the bowl and knock it down. (You are expelling the air caused by the rising.) If the dough seems sticky to the touch, you can lightly flour your board. If dry (not silky), spritz on a little water. Knead again. When you've got the look and feel of a baby's butt, fold under two sides of the dough, creating a loaf shape, and place it in the pan. Return it to its cozy place to rise again. It should double in size in about ½ hour.

Beat the other egg with 1 tablespoon of milk to create a glaze and brush it on the top of the bread. Bake it in the middle of the oven for 40 minutes (while you talk to the prospective buyers of your house!), until the crust is golden brown. When the bread is done, you can easily roll it out of the pan onto a clean dish towel and thump on the bottom with your index finger. If you get a hollow sound, the bread is perfectly done. If you get a dull thud, put the bread back into the pan and bake for a little while longer.

Let the bread cool for 10 minutes in the pan and for another 10 minutes out of the pan. Slice with a bread knife, using a saw motion to avoid smushing your beautiful bread. Give a piece with some jam to those people who just agreed to your asking price for the house.

Cinnamon-Swirl Bread

Makes 1 loaf

This is the bread we use at the restaurant to make our Cinnamon-Swirl French Toast. It is made using the recipe for the White Bread dough.

1 recipe for White Bread (preceding)
2 tablespoons sugar
1 teaspoon cinnamon
3 tablespoons butter, melted

Follow the recipe for White Bread, remembering the butter you will need for your pan and the egg and milk for the glazing.

Mix the cinnamon into the sugar.

After the first rise of the dough, roll it out to ⅜ inch thickness, with the objective of fashioning a carpet 8½ x 12 inches in dimensions. Work the corners by pushing with your fingers. Be very careful not to rip the dough.

Brush the surface of the dough with the melted butter and then sprinkle the cinnamon-sugar *evenly* over the buttered dough. Now you are going to roll the 12-inch length of the dough tightly, leaving no slack space in the swirl. You don't want any pockets of air in the roll.

Start the roll with your fingertips, and as you roll make sure to push in at the seam where the bottom of the dough is meeting the cinnamon-sugar. Continue carefully, pulling the dough back to its original 8½-inch width as it tries to shrink on you. When you reach the end, pinch the two layers of dough together to anchor the end of the dough in a kind of suture to the body of the roll. The swirl (or spiral) you see at the ends of the roll will move from center to second layer to third and final layer.

Place the bread roll, suture side down, in your buttered bread pan and let it rise for ½ hour in its warm spot. After the dough has doubled in size, brush the glaze of beaten egg and milk over the top. Bake as you would the White Bread for 40 minutes.

You must let the bread cool—10 minutes in the pan, 10 minutes out—and cut it carefully with a bread knife. We have enjoyed 20 years of fame using this bread to make our Cinnamon-Swirl French Toast (p. 64).

Whole-Wheat Bread

Makes 1 loaf

If you are in the mood to make a substantial, healthful meal out of a thick slice of homemade bread, this is the one for you. We use it for our Hole-in-the-Bread (p. 25).

1¾ cups whole-wheat flour
½ cup all-purpose flour
½ cup ground oats
1 packet dry yeast
1 cup plus 2 tablespoons warm water
1 tablespoon molasses
2 tablespoons whole plain yogurt
2 tablespoons melted butter, plus some soft for the pan
1 teaspoon salt
½ teaspoon baking soda
1 teaspoon vegetable oil
1 egg plus a few drops of water for the glaze

Notice that there is no egg in this recipe, with the exception of the glaze.

Mix the flours and oats together and warm them in the oven at 350 degrees for about 10 minutes. (I think I got this from James Beard. It must help the action of the yeast.)

Make your sponge by putting the yeast into 2 tablespoons of warm (to the wrist) water with a few drops of the molasses. The sponge should grow in 3 to 5 minutes.

Mix the yogurt together with the molasses and let it warm near a pilot light before combining it with the melted butter.

Now combine your warmed flour mixture with the salt and baking soda in the standing mixer set for low speed using the dough hook. Make sure they are well mixed—a clump of baking soda can be deadly! Add the yogurt-molasses-butter mixture and beat into the flour. Stop the mixer and use a rubber spatula to scrape down the sides.

Add the sponge and the cup of warm water and mix to incorporate evenly throughout the dough. (Stop the mixer and scrape down anything from the sides if you need to.) When your dough ball seems smooth and silky and will bounce back from an intrusive thumb, remove it to the board.

If the dough is sticky, you'll probably have a little flour in the bottom of the mixer bowl to use for flouring your board. Knead the dough, pushing it with the heels of your hands toward the center, to ensure its silky, resilient perfection.

Place the dough in a glass bowl with the teaspoon of vegetable oil and roll the dough to coat it lightly with the oil. Cover with a towel and set it in a warm (65–75 degrees), draft-free spot to rise until it doubles in size (about 1 hour).

After the first rise, knock the dough down and knead away the oiliness and restore a silky surface to the dough. Tuck under two sides, forming a loaf, and place it in the buttered bread pan, tuck side down. Cover and return to its warm spot for ½ hour, during which it should again double in size.

Preheat the oven to 400 degrees. (You can't have the dough near the oven now if it's still rising.) Whisk the egg well with a couple drops of water and use this to brush over the top of the dough once it has finished rising.

When the oven has reached its temperature, put the bread on the center of the middle rack. Turn the temperature down to 350 degrees and bake for about 40 minutes.

When you think the bread is ready, take it out of the oven and roll it out of the pan onto its side on a clean dish towel. Thump the bottom of the bread with a finger. If you hear a hollow sound, the bread is done. Let it cool for 10 to 15 minutes before slicing.

7-Grain Bread

Makes 1 loaf

We soak the oats, wheat germ, cornmeal, and buckwheat overnight in the refrigerator to encourage it to germinate before using it in this recipe. This enhances the flavor and probably the usable vitamin content as well. So plan the night before, if you're baking this bread. Since it involves this extra degree of preparation, you might want to make a couple of loaves. Store them in the refrigerator. This is a very hearty, flavorful bread.

4 tablespoons rolled oats
4 tablespoons wheat germ
4 tablespoons cornmeal
3 tablespoons buckwheat
4 tablespoons water (for soaking the above grains)
1 packet dry yeast
½ cup warm water (for yeast)
¼ cup molasses
¼ cup yogurt
4 tablespoons raw sunflower seeds
2 teaspoons gluten
2 teaspoons salt
½ cup whole-wheat flour
1½ cups all-purpose flour
1 teaspoon vegetable oil

Mix the oats, wheat germ, cornmeal, and buckwheat with 4 tablespoons or enough water to completely soak the grain with no excess. A glass container is best for this because you can spot any dry pockets of grain. Cover with plastic wrap and leave in the refrigerator overnight.

The next day put the yeast into the warm water with ½ teaspoon of the molasses to grow the sponge (3 to 5 minutes). Stir the rest of the molasses into the yogurt and set it near a pilot light to warm up for 5 minutes.

Combine the dry ingredients—the sunflower seeds, gluten, salt, and one-third of each of the flours—in the mixer at low speed, then add the mixture from the refrigerator and blend well. Always stop the mixer after combining ingredients and scrape down the sides with your spatula.

Add the warmed yogurt-molasses mixture and beat to combine. Now put in the yeast sponge, mix it in, and add the rest of the flour. Run the mixer until everything is fully combined and the dough looks uniform in texture and balls up around the dough hook.

Remove the dough from the mixer bowl and flour the board with the little left in the mixer bowl. (You'll probably need to, as this dough is sticky.) Knead the dough until it is silky and resilient.

Put the dough in a glass bowl with the vegetable oil and roll it around to coat it. Cover with a towel and put in a warm (110-degree) place to rise until double in bulk (45 minutes to 1 hour).

Knock the dough down and knead again. Tuck under two sides to make a loaf and place in a buttered bread pan, seam side down. Cover again and let rise for ½ hour. Place on middle rack of 400-degree oven, turn the heat down to 350, and bake 40 minutes to 1 hour, or until golden brown.

Let the bread cool for 15 minutes before slicing. Like the Whole-Wheat Bread, you can make a meal of this bread.

Note: Gluten is a component of flour. It is added when flours from dark grains are used to assist the yeast action. It can be purchased in health food and specialty stores.

American French Bread

Makes 2 loaves with chef, 1 without

Knowing the French very well, I hesitated to call my bread French bread, so I'm calling it American, or perhaps I should spell it américain. Whatever! . . . as they say in the Valley. You can make this recipe without first making a chef the day before, but I hope you will try the chef—it makes a difference, particularly with this deceptively simple bread.

½ pound chef dough, if using
2 teaspoons dry yeast
⅔ cup warm water
¼ teaspoon sugar (for the sponge)
2½ cups all-purpose flour
1½ teaspoons salt
2 tablespoons olive oil plus 1 teaspoon for dough bowl
1 egg (for glazing)
Spritzer with water (a plant mister)

To make the chef you would make one recipe of this dough, and after it has risen once, knock it down, wrap in plastic wrap, and store in the refrigerator. It will keep for about 48 hours. If you slice this quantity in half, each portion will be roughly ½ pound.

In a glass or ceramic bowl, mix the yeast with 2 tablespoons of the warm water and the sugar. Let it sit for 3 to 5 minutes while the sponge grows.

Put 2 cups of the flour with the salt in the mixer bowl and combine at the lowest speed. Reserve ½ cup of the flour—if it is humid you will probably have to add some. With the mixer still on low, add 2 tablespoons of olive oil and the rest of the warm water.

Now add the sponge and increase the mixer speed one notch. Watch the dough. When almost all the flour is incorporated, stop the mixer and scrape down the sides with your spatula, then add the ½ pound of chef if you're using it. Beat on the next higher speed until both doughs are as one—silky and smooth.

If you're not using a chef, or if the dough you're making is going to be the chef, just continue beating until the dough is silky and smooth. You may have to add a little flour at this time if the dough is sticky.

Take the dough and if need be, lightly flour the board before putting the dough on it. Knead the dough with the heels of your hands, adding flour or spritzing with water to get the silky, resilient surface you're looking for.

Swirl the 1 teaspoon of olive oil around the glass rising bowl, place the dough in it, and coat completely. Cover the dough with a towel and place in a warm (110 degrees) spot with no drafts and let it double in size. Once it has risen, you can knock it down and wrap it up as a chef or go on to the next step.

If you have used the chef, you will have enough dough for two loaves. Roll the dough with your hands into a large cigar shape approximately 12 inches by 1½ inches. Cut the dough in half. (Don't rip!) Now make 2 equal-sized cigars. Hopefully your board is in a nice warm spot; if not, the loaves need to go back to the rising spot to double in size once more (about 30 minutes).

Preheat your oven to 400 degrees. Glaze the loaves with the egg beaten with a couple drops of water. With a sharp knife make three shallow slashes across the center third of the loaves. Steady the loaves with a hand while you do this and don't cut yourself!

Place the loaves on a baking sheet dusted with a little cornmeal and put them in the middle of the center rack of the oven to bake. Spritz the loaves with your mister (or mist your loaves with your spritzer) 3 times during baking, which should be about 20 minutes. Voilà! *Pain français à l'américain!*

My favorite *petit déjeuner* when I was a student in Aix-en-Provence was a piece of French bread with butter and jam, which I would dip, bread-butter-and-jam, into my café au lait.

Challah

Makes 1 loaf

Challah is a textured, unsweet egg bread that can be made with either three or six braids. It is traditionally served on the Jewish sabbath. For a festive brunch dish, see the recipe for Challah Hole-in-the-Bread with Grand Marnier Bananas on page 66.

1 packet dry yeast
2 tablespoons plus ½ teaspoon sugar
¼ cup warm water (110 degrees)
6 tablespoons (¾ stick) butter
1 cup milk
1½ teaspoons salt
4¼ to 4¾ cups all-purpose flour
3 eggs (1 for the glaze)
3 teaspoons vegetable oil

Put the yeast together with the ½ teaspoon sugar and the warm water in a glass or ceramic bowl and let sit for 3 to 5 minutes.

Melt the butter together with the milk in a small saucepan until the milk bubbles around the edges (scalds).

In the standing mixer with the dough hook combine the 2 tablespoons of sugar, the salt, and 4 cups of the flour at lowest speed. Now add the scalded milk and butter and beat for 1 minute. Whisk 2 of the eggs in a separate container and add to the mixer. Beat together on next higher speed. Stop the mixer and scrape down the sides with your spatula.

Add ½ cup more flour along with the yeast sponge and beat together until silky smooth. Stop the mixer once and run the spatula down the sides of the bowl to check for any vagrant dry mix.

Knead the Challah dough on a very lightly floured board until it bounces back from a thumb impression and is totally smooth. Put the dough in a glass bowl with 2 teaspoons of the vegetable oil; coat the dough with the oil, cover with a towel, and set in a warm place to rise until doubled in bulk (1 to 1½ hours).

Bring the dough back to the board and knock it down (or punch it down—depending on your mood). Cut the dough into 3 equal parts. Knead them until smooth, and set them on a greased cookie sheet to rise for another 20 minutes.

Preheat the oven to 350 degrees. Whisk the third egg with a teaspoon of vegetable oil for glazing.

Knock down the doughs and roll them with your hands into three "snakes" about 2 inches thick and 17 inches long, tapering a little at the ends. Push gently to elongate the dough—you don't want to tear it. Lay the "snakes" side-by-side, not quite touching. Crimp the three snake tails together. To braid, alternately move the outside braids over the center one—left over, right over, left over—until you come to the end. (Most women know how to do this. The men may want to practice with three strands of rope beforehand.) Braid tightly—you don't want any gaps—and crimp the ends together.

Place the braided Challah on a greased cookie sheet and paint it lavishly with the glaze—don't miss a single spot! Bake in the center of the oven for 30 to 40 minutes, until uniformly golden. Thump on the bottom of the bread and listen for the hollow sound that tells you the bread is done.

Let the Challah cool a bit before slicing, and save some for Challah Hole-in-the-Bread.

Cracquelin (Belgian Sugar Bread)

Makes 1 loaf

Growing up in Belgium, I would go to the bakery every Sunday for a loaf of cracquelin (sugar bread) or cramique (raisin bread). They are wonderful toasted and eaten with a little butter on top. You will need a springform pan for this recipe and the next.

½ cup plus 1 tablespoon scalded milk
1 packet dry yeast
½ cup warm water plus pinch of sugar
3 to 3½ cups all-purpose flour
3 tablespoons sugar
1 teaspoon salt
3 eggs (separate 1, discard white; reserve 1 for glaze)
8 tablespoons (1 stick) soft butter (reserve 1 tablespoon
  for pan)
1 cup crystallized sugar (the translucent, rock-candy sort)

Bring milk to a scald, then remove and let cool for 5 minutes.

Put the yeast into the warm water with the pinch of sugar and stir with a wooden spoon. Let sit for 5 minutes.

Mix together in an ungreased bowl: the ½ cup of warmed milk, the yeast sponge, and 1 cup of the flour. Let this "starter" rise, covered, in a warm place for 1 hour, until doubled in size.

In the bowl of the standing mixer fitted with the paddle attachment, put 2 cups of flour, the 3 tablespoons of sugar, and the salt. Combine at low speed. Beat 1 egg and 1 yolk and add it plus the starter dough to the mixer. Increase mixer speed a notch and beat together. Now add 7 tablespoons of the butter gradually, bit by bit. It is best to have little pieces of butter dispersed through the dough.

When the dough comes together around the paddle, stop the mixer and scrape down the sides, looking for any unassimilated pockets of dry mix. If you find any, break them up with the spatula and beat again until the dough is soft and slightly sticky.

Add a little flour to your board and knead until the dough is no longer sticky. Cut off a section of dough to make a ball the size of a baseball. Roll this ball out until it is about 9 inches in diameter.

Reserve about 2 tablespoons of the crystallized sugar and knead the rest into the larger piece of dough. Keep the dough round, but fashion a little base for it to sit on. Place the ball of dough in the center of the rolled-out dough and gather this up, creating a cup around the larger ball. Now put your dough into the springform pan greased with the remaining table-spoon of butter and cover with a clean towel to rise again for 1½ hours, until doubled in size.

Preheat the oven to 350 degrees. Beat the last egg together with the remaining 1 tablespoon of warmed milk for glazing.

Once the dough has risen, brush a generous amount of glaze on it. Make a circle of slashes on the top of the dough and sprinkle the rest of the crystal sugar. Place in the center of the oven and bake for 25 to 30 minutes. Check for done-ness by removing the bread from the pan and tapping the bottom with your index finger. If you hear a hollow sound, the bread's done.

Let the Cracquelin cool in the pan for 15 minutes before removing to slice.

Cramique (Raisin Bread)

Makes 1 loaf

Good Enough to Eat is so well known for serving American home-style food that I suppose I could have dropped the Belgian names for these breads, but I grew up in Belgium and I wanted to credit the origin of the recipes. My restaurant is analogous to New York City: American with many nationalities. An oxy-moron that works!

1 recipe for Cracquelin dough (preceding recipe, but
    without crystallized sugar)
1 cup water (to poach the raisins)
1 cup dark raisins
1 tea bag

Prepare the dough according to the preceding recipe.

Prior to the second rising, boil the cup of water in a saucepan, add the raisins, bring to a second boil, and remove from the heat. Add the tea bag, let it steep for 1 minute, and remove. Cover the pan and let sit to cool.

When the water is cool enough to stick your finger in, drain it from the raisins. Pat the raisins dry with a paper towel.

Now, you have just rolled out your "baseball" of dough. Knead the raisins as delicately as you can into the larger piece of dough, trying to disperse them evenly throughout. This is the same stage at which you kneaded in the crystallized sugar. Now proceed as you would for the Cracquelin, creating a round loaf to cup inside the 9-inch disk . . . into the buttered springform pan . . . second rising . . . glaze . . . bake . . . *et voilà*: Cramique! (Rhymes with Monique.)

Potato-Basil Bread

Makes 1 big loaf

This is a large, free-form, herbed bread fit for a large family. If your family happens to number under six, invite the relatives or neighbors over for a farm-style buffet brunch, and put this bread in the center of the table.

1 cup mashed potatoes
1 packet dry yeast
Pinch sugar
½ cup warm (110 degrees) water
1 cup buttermilk
¼ cup (½ stick) soft butter plus 2 tablespoons for
    baking sheet
⅛ teaspoon white pepper
Pinch nutmeg
3 tablespoons fresh basil leaves, chiffonade, or cut into
    thin strips
6 to 7 cups all-purpose flour
1 tablespoon salt
1 tablespoon vegetable oil for rising bowl
1 egg and 1 tablespoon milk for glaze

Peel 1 large or 2 small potatoes, boil until tender, drain, and mash.

Make the sponge: yeast plus sugar plus ½ cup warm water; stir with a plastic or wooden spoon. Let sit 3 to 5 minutes.

In a saucepan bring to a scald the buttermilk, ¼ cup butter, white pepper, nutmeg, and 1 tablespoon of the basil.

Combine the flour with the salt in a large bowl, then transfer 5 cups of the flour to the bowl of your standing mixer fitted with the dough hook. Add the mashed potatoes and the buttermilk scald, and beat together. Stop the mixer and scrape down anything from the sides. Add the sponge and 1 more cup of flour along with the rest of the basil. Beat until the dough starts to come together over the dough hook.

Scrape down the sides of the mixer bowl and check for any pockets of dry ingredients with the spatula. Beat a little more, then check the dough. If it is sticky, add small amounts of flour and beat until silky and smooth.

Remove the dough to the board, flour only if needed, and knead until the dough is elastic and will bounce back from a thumb impression. Place in a large glass bowl with the table-spoon of vegetable oil and coat the dough with the oil before covering with a clean dish towel and transferring to a warm spot to rise until doubled (1 hour).

Knock the dough down, knead a bit more to get rid of the oiliness and return the dough to its smooth and silky texture. Flour only if needed. Put the dough on a large buttered baking sheet and return to the warm spot to rise again: 30 to 40 minutes, to double.

Now here's a notion: If you have eight bricks kicking around somewhere, put them in the oven on the middle rack, creating a platform for your baking sheet. Turn the oven on and preheat to 350 degrees. I've tried this and somehow the bread comes out better. (Don't despair if you haven't got any bricks; the bread will still be great!)

Beat the egg and tablespoon of milk together and brush onto the bread. With a sharp knife, slash a tick-tack-toe pat-tern on the top of the bread. Put the bread pan on the bricks and bake for 20 to 25 minutes, until nicely browned. Take the bread out of the pan and thump on the bottom, listening for a hollow sound, to check for doneness.

Let the bread cool for 10 minutes before slicing. Serve warm with some butter. Try to time the bread so it comes out of the oven just when the neighbors are arriving.

Pumpkin Bread

Makes 1 loaf

This bread is made at the restaurant in the fall and winter, and we offer a French toast made with it. Although the cow is the symbol by which we are known, it could as easily have been a turkey or a pumpkin. Our busiest part of the year is in the fall, and when the pumpkins hit the markets, we know it's time to get ready for the crowds.

Pumpkin Bread is rich and spicy and one of the reasons to give thanks.

1 packet dry yeast
Pinch sugar
¼ cup warm water
3 to 4 cups flour
1 teaspoon cinnamon
½ teaspoon ginger
¼ teaspoon cloves
½ teaspoon allspice
1 teaspoon salt
5 tablespoons melted butter (3 for dough, 1 for rising, 1 for pan)
⅓ cup warm milk
1 cup pumpkin puree
¼ cup brown sugar
2 eggs (1 reserve, plus 1 tablespoon milk, for glaze)
½ cup raisins (optional)
½ cup chopped walnuts (optional)

Combine the yeast and pinch of sugar in the warm water and let the sponge brew for 3 to 5 minutes.

In the bowl of the standing mixer fitted with the dough hook, combine 3 cups of the flour with the spices and salt. Mix 3 tablespoons of the butter, warm milk, pumpkin puree, and the brown sugar together in a bowl, then add it to the mixer and beat. Stop the mixer. Scrape down the sides and add 1 egg (beaten separately). After the egg is beaten in, add the sponge and beat until the dough comes together around the dough hook.

Stop the mixer and scrape down the sides to see that all the dry ingredients are incorporated into the dough. You may have some residue at the bottom of the mixer—don't worry about that, you can use it for flouring and kneading. If the dough seems sticky, add a little flour and beat until it becomes silky and resilient.

Put the dough on your board and roll it out into a thick circle. Spread the raisins and nuts (if you're using them) over the dough and then knead them in. Be careful not to tear the dough. Shape the dough into a ball and put it into a glass bowl with a tablespoon of melted butter. Roll the dough to coat it with butter, cover with a towel, and set in a warm (65 to 75 degrees), draft-free spot to rise until double in size (about 1 hour).

Knock down the dough and knead until silky and smooth. Form the dough into a loaf shape, pushing in the sides, and put it in the buttered loaf pan, seam side down. Put the pan in the warm spot and let the dough again double in size (30 minutes).

Preheat the oven to 350 degrees. Beat the second egg and the tablespoon of milk together and glaze the risen loaf. Put the pan in the oven in the center of the middle rack and bake for 45 to 50 minutes, rotating the pan twice during cooking.

When the bread is a toasty, chestnut color, take it out of the oven and tip it out of the pan onto a clean dish towel. Thump on the bottom with your index finger. If you hear a hollow sound, the bread is done. (This is the only surefire way I have found to test doneness.) If it doesn't sound hollow, return it to the pan and the oven.

Let the Pumpkin Bread cool in the pan for 10 minutes and out of the pan for another 10. Slice with a bread knife. If you keep it around for a day or two, it will have dried out somewhat and be perfect for Pumpkin Bread French Toast (p. 62).

Cocoa-Chocolate Bread

Makes 1 loaf

This is a breakfast bread for fans of chocolate. It makes a wonderful baked bread pudding soaked in the French Toast custard (p. 61) with an extra egg and a couple tablespoons of Jamaican rum. Use Callebaut cocoa and chocolate if you can find it. It is the richest (the best!) I know of.

1 packet dry yeast
Pinch sugar
¼ cup warm water
½ cup milk plus 1 tablespoon for the glaze
4 tablespoons butter, soft (reserve 1 tablespoon for the rising bowl; 1 tablespoon for the pan)
2½ cups all-purpose flour
¼ cup Callebaut cocoa
½ teaspoon salt
1 tablespoon dark brown sugar
1 tablespoon white sugar
2 eggs (1 for the glaze)
3 ounces (½ cup) Callebaut semisweet chocolate tablets (broken into small pieces)

Stir the yeast together with the pinch of sugar into the warm water with a wooden spoon and set in a warm place to foam up a sponge.

In a small saucepan scald the ½ cup milk together with 2 tablespoons of the butter. Once it bubbles around the edges, remove from heat.

Put the flour, cocoa, salt, and sugars into the mixer bowl and combine at low speed with the dough hook. Add the milk-butter mixture and 1 egg (beaten separately) to the mixer bowl and beat to combine. Stop the mixer to scrape down whatever has spattered up the sides of the mixer bowl.

Add the sponge and beat together until the dough comes together around the dough hook. Stop the mixer and use the spatula to again scrape down the sides and look for any unassimilated dry ingredients. Beat a little more, if need be.

Take the dough out of the mixer and knead on your board, flouring a little if the dough is sticky. Once the dough is silky to the touch, put it in a glass bowl with 1 tablespoon of melted butter. Roll the dough to coat it with butter. Cover with a dish towel and set in a warm, draft-free place to rise until doubled (about 1 hour).

Knock down the dough on your board and roll it out. Scatter the pieces of chocolate over the dough and knead to incorporate. When the dough is silky once more, form a loaf shape, tucking in at the sides, and place it in a buttered loaf pan, seam side down. Let it rise for about 30 minutes, until doubled in bulk.

Preheat the oven to 350 degrees. Beat the remaining egg together with the 1 tablespoon of milk and brush it over the loaf. Place in the middle of the center rack and bake for 40 minutes, turning the pan once. Check the bread by removing it from the pan and tapping on the bottom: If it doesn't sound hollow, it's not done—back into the oven!

Let the bread cool 10 minutes in the pan and 10 minutes out before slicing.

Muffins, Scones, and Biscuits

Twenty years ago, my husband, Bill, and I went on an excursion on his motorcycle to Provincetown, Massachusetts. We had breakfast one morning at a restaurant called Poor Richard's Buttery. Along with some scrambled eggs, I ordered what turned out to be the perfect peach muffin. I will never forget it: large, mushroomed, crunchy cinnamon-sugar dome; airy inside, with juicy chunks of peach. The baker who made that muffin wasn't there, and even if I had had his recipe, I don't know if I would have been able to duplicate the transcendental magic of that muffin. From that moment on, I was like Parsifal searching for the answer to the riddle of the Grail King.

There is something mystical about muffins, scones, and biscuits. For years I've puzzled over the nuances of baking them: how some bakers whom I've worked with just seem to have a "touch" that produces the perfect muffin. Although no two bakers will produce identical muffins or scones or biscuits, the good ones seem to have a kind of spiritual need built into them—they're always seeking the "perfect muffin."

These recipes are my effort to part the shrouds of mystery. All the baked goods served at Good Enough to Eat are made in the restaurant according to my recipes. In my twenty-plus years of experimenting and testing, there's one thing that stands out as critical for successful baking: *how you blend the ingredients!* Also, treat baking as a precise science: follow the recipes and techniques carefully, and be sure your oven is calibrated correctly.

MUFFINS

A food processor is the way to go for these recipes, and of course you need a 12-cup muffin pan made for 2½-inch liners. You can get fewer but larger muffins with broad, crunchy tops by filling the muffin liners to the top. The batter will rise and spread over the top of the pan, so you must use a knife to score between the muffins before removing. Also, baking on the top rack of the oven helps make those muffin domes crunchier.

Peach-Mango Muffins

Makes 12 muffins

8 tablespoons (½ cup, or 1 stick) cold butter, plus a little
    to grease the muffin pan
1½ teaspoons cinnamon
½ cup plus 3 tablespoons sugar
1½ cups peaches, peeled and cut into ½-inch chunks
1 cup ripe mango, peeled and cut into ½-inch chunks
2 teaspoons lemon juice
1½ cups all-purpose flour
½ teaspoon salt
1 tablespoon baking powder
1 egg
¾ cup milk
1 teaspoon pure vanilla extract

Preheat the oven to 350 degrees. Grease the top of your muffin pan with a little butter to prevent the muffin domes from sticking. Put the muffin liners into the pan.

Blend the cinnamon and the 3 tablespoons of sugar together in a small bowl. In a larger bowl, mix the fruit together with 1½ tablespoons of the cinnamon-sugar and the 2 teaspoons of lemon juice.

In another bowl, mix together the flour, salt, and baking powder. Beat the egg in your measuring cup and then combine it with the milk and vanilla. Cut the 8 tablespoons of butter into pats (the size you get in the diner with a paper on top).

Put the pats of butter in the food processor and add the ½ cup of sugar. Pulse until mixed but still lumpy. Push down whatever is clinging to the sides of the processor with a rubber spatula between all pulsing sessions.

Now add the dry and liquid ingredients—pulsing, scraping down, and adding, in that order—in the following sequence: one-third dry (pulse twice to blend), one-half liquid (pulse twice), one-third dry (pulse twice), one-half liquid (pulse twice), one-third dry (pulse twice). Caution: *Do not pulse* while you are scraping down the sides or when you are adding ingredients!

The batter should still appear slightly lumpy—it is important not to overmix! Finally, put in the fruit and pulse a few times to mix it into the batter.

Pour the batter into the muffin pan, filling the liners to just below their top edges. Sprinkle the remaining 1½ tablespoons of cinnamon-sugar over the tops of the muffins.

Bake in the oven for 20 to 25 minutes, turning the pan once. You can check for doneness with a fork—when the tines come out clean and dry, the muffins are done.

Let the muffins cool for 10 minutes or so before removing them from the pan. The aroma that fills the house is blissful, and if a crowd doesn't form in the kitchen area during that 10 minutes, you must live alone!

Orange-Date Muffins

Makes 8 muffins

You can make Cherry–Chocolate Chip Muffins *with this recipe* *by substituting ¾ cup of chopped sour cherries for the orange* *and 4 ounces of semisweet chocolate chips for the dates.*

1 large or 2 small oranges (6 ounces total weight)
1 egg
1 cup milk
1 teaspoon pure vanilla extract
2½ cups all-purpose flour
½ teaspoon salt
1 tablespoon baking powder
¾ cup sugar
4 tablespoons (¼ cup, or ½ stick) soft butter (not cold)
1 cup (8 ounces) dates, pitted and chopped into small
  pieces

Preheat oven to 350 degrees. Grease the top of your muffin pan with a little butter to prevent the muffin domes from sticking. Put the muffin liners in the pan.

Zest half of the large orange (or one whole orange if you're using two). Remember to avoid getting any of the white part of the orange in the zest. Now section the orange into suprèmes (see p. 191). Do the sectioning over a bowl in order to catch the juice, which you reserve with the sections.

Beat the egg in your measuring cup, and combine it with the milk and vanilla. Mix the flour, salt, and baking powder in a large bowl. Mix well—you want the baking powder evenly distributed in the flour.

Combine the sugar and butter by pulsing it in the food processor for a few seconds. It should stay a little lumpy.

Now add the dry and liquid ingredients to the processor as described in the Peach-Mango Muffins recipe (p. 106): one-third dry (pulse twice, stop, scrape down), one-half liquid (pulse twice, stop, scrape down), one-third dry, and so on, until you have combined the dry and liquid ingredients with the sugar-butter mixture. Finally, pulse in the orange sections, with their juice and zest, and the dates just enough to distribute them evenly in the batter.

Pour the batter into the lined muffin cups, leaving a scant ⅛ inch of the upper edge of the liners above the batter. Bake for 20 to 25 minutes, turning the pan once after 15 minutes or so. Test for doneness by pricking with a fork. If done, the tines will be clean and dry.

Let the muffins cool for 10 minutes before taking them out of the pan. If you try to take them out sooner, when they're very hot, they are more likely to break apart.

Strawberry-Coconut Muffins

Makes 12 muffins

2 eggs
2 cups all-purpose flour (sifted after measuring)
¼ teaspoon baking soda
1 teaspoon baking powder
¼ teaspoon salt
1½ cups very ripe strawberries, sliced
1 teaspoon lemon juice
1 teaspoon pure vanilla extract
⅔ cup sugar
8 tablespoons (½ cup, or 1 stick) soft butter
¼ teaspoon cream of tartar
½ cup buttermilk
1 cup sweetened coconut shreds

Preheat oven to 325 degrees. Lightly grease the top of your muffin pan with some butter. Put the muffin liners into the muffin pan.

Separate the eggs. Mix the flour, baking soda, baking powder, and salt together in a large bowl. Toss the strawberries with the lemon juice in a bowl. Beat the vanilla with the egg yolks in your mixing cup.

In the food processor cream the sugar and butter until white. Next, pulse in the egg yolks and vanilla mixture.

Whip the egg whites with the cream of tartar until they hold a soft peak.

Add half of the dry mix to the processor and pulse about three times to blend. Now pour in the buttermilk and pulse. Put the rest of the dry mix in and pulse again. Remember to scrape down the sides of the processor after each addition-pulse sequence—and never add anything to the processor while it is pulsing.

Remove the batter from the processor with your spatula into a large bowl. Fold the coconut and strawberries into the batter. Lastly, fold in the egg whites in a horizontal figure-eight pattern, turning the bowl three or four times while you're doing it.

Pour the batter into the muffin cups, filling them up to the edge of the liners. Bake 25 to 30 minutes, turning the pan after 15 minutes. Test to see if they're done with a fork—clean, dry tines mean "done."

Let the muffins cool for 10 minutes before trying to lift them out of the pan.

Note: You can substitute raspberries for the strawberries to make (you guessed it!) Raspberry-Coconut Muffins.

Granola Muffins

Makes 10 to 12 muffins

We make this muffin at the restaurant with our own Granola (p. 71), which has quite a bit of honey in it. If you substitute your own favorite cereal and it isn't sweetened already, you may want to add a little more sugar to this recipe.

1 cup all-purpose flour
⅓ cup whole-wheat flour
1 cup granola
1 teaspoon baking powder
½ teaspoon baking soda
½ teaspoon salt
¼ cup (4 ounces, ½ stick) soft butter
¼ cup dark brown sugar
1 egg
⅓ cup honey
1 cup plain yogurt (whole milk)
1 cup dried apricots, chopped into ¼-inch pieces

Preheat the oven to 350 degrees. Lightly grease the top of your muffin pan with some butter. Put the muffin liners into the pan.

Put the flours, granola, baking powder, baking soda, and salt in a large bowl and mix well.

Using the food processor, cream the butter and sugar together until light and fluffy. Having beaten the egg well in your measuring cup, pulse to combine it with the butter and sugar. Then add the honey and yogurt, pulsing to combine. Next, pulse in the dry ingredients. Lastly, pulse in the apricots just enough to completely distribute them throughout the batter.

Pour the batter into the muffin pan almost to the top edge of each muffin cup. Bake in the oven for 25 to 30 minutes, turning once. Test for doneness with the fork tines.

Let the muffins cool for 10 minutes before lifting them out of the pan.

Raisin-Bran Muffins

Makes about 9 muffins

1 cup all-purpose flour
1⅓ cups bran
1 teaspoon baking soda
¼ cup dark brown sugar (pack down for measure)
¼ cup (4 ounces, ½ stick) soft butter
1 egg
½ cup molasses
1 cup sour cream
1 cup raisins

Preheat the oven to 350 degrees. Lightly grease the top of your muffin pan with some butter to prevent sticking. Put the muffin liners in the pan cups.

Mix the flour, bran, and baking soda together in a large bowl.

Using the food processor, cream the brown sugar and butter together. (Nary a speck of sugar should show.) Beat the egg well in your measuring cup and combine it with the molasses and sour cream in a bowl.

Now, alternately pulse the flour mixture and the sour cream mixture into the sugar-butter mixture in the following manner: one-third dry mix (pulse, stop, scrape down the sides of the processor), one-half sour cream mix (pulse, stop, scrape down), and so on, until all mixes are completely blended. Finally, pulse in the raisins enough to distribute them evenly in the batter.

Pour the batter into the muffin cups, filling almost to the top of the paper liners, and bake for 30 minutes, turning the pan after 15 minutes. Check for doneness with the tines of a fork toward the end of the cooking time—dry tines mean done muffins!

Let the muffins cool for 10 minutes before removing them from the pan.

Espresso–Chocolate Chip Muffins

Makes 12 muffins, or 18 with smaller-cup muffin pan

These muffins are very rich and sweet and are nice to serve instead of cookies at teatime. I do suggest that you make the smaller muffins if you have the pan and liners for them. To make them festive, cut stencils of stars, hearts, crescent moons, and so on, out of parchment or waxed paper sized to fit at the center of each muffin. Lay them on the finished muffins and dust with confectioners' sugar, then carefully remove to leave the silhouettes of the stencils on the muffins. It's a Martha Stewart kind of thing!

8 tablespoons (½ cup, or 1 stick) softened butter
1¾ cups dark brown sugar (lightly packed for measuring)
3 eggs
2 teaspoons pure vanilla extract
1 cup sour cream
½ cup triple-strength espresso
2¼ cups all-purpose flour
½ cup unsweetened cocoa
½ teaspoon salt
2 teaspoons baking soda
1 cup semisweet chocolate chips
Confectioners' sugar

Preheat the oven to 350 degrees. Lightly butter the top surface of the muffin pans and put in the muffin liners.

Beat the butter in the food processor until it is white. Add the brown sugar and beat it into the butter.

Beat the eggs in a measuring cup, then combine with the vanilla, sour cream, and espresso in a bowl or your measuring cup, if it is large enough.

In another bowl, combine the flour, cocoa, salt, and baking soda.

Now combine the dry and liquid ingredients with the

sugar-butter mixture in the food processor by thirds (dry) and halves: Add one-third dry (pulse, stop, scrape down sides of processor), one-half liquid (pulse, stop, scrape down), and so on, until completely mixed. Remember to stop the processor before scraping down and adding the fractional amounts.

Finally, add the chocolate chips, pulsing just enough to distribute them evenly throughout the batter.

Pour the batter into the muffin pans, filling to just a smidge under the edge of the liners, and bake for 25 to 30 minutes, turning once after 15 minutes. Use a fork to check to see if they're done—dry tines mean done muffins!

Let the muffins cool completely before removing them from the pans and dusting with confectioners' sugar or applying the silhouette stencils.

SCONES

My epiphany with the scone came in the late '70s while at a little restaurant overlooking the white cliffs of Dover. I was living in England at the time and going to Pru Leith's School of Food and Wine in London. My friend and I had traveled down to Dover for the weekend.

It was about four in the afternoon, and following the tradition, we stopped at this place for tea. The tea came with a warm currant scone (the English pronounce it "skahn"), and it was served with strawberry jam and clotted cream. At the first bite, I was afloat in the blue skies, carried over the white cliffs, totally blissed by the taste of that scone and the smell of the sea. Also, I believe that at the time I was getting on quite well with my English boyfriend.

My scones come pretty close to the one I had in Dover, although mine are made with buttermilk and are triangular instead of round.

Carrie's Scones

Makes 8 scones

4 tablespoons (¼ cup, or ½ stick) cold butter
2 cups all-purpose flour
½ teaspoon salt
1 tablespoon baking powder
¼ teaspoon baking soda
¼ cup sugar
2 eggs (1 for glazing)
½ cup buttermilk

Preheat the oven to 350 degrees.

Take the butter out of the refrigerator and cut it into small chunks, around ¼-inch cubes. Wrap the butter chunks in the butter paper again and return them to the refrigerator.

In a large bowl, mix all the dry ingredients, including the sugar. In a separate bowl or your measuring cup, beat 1 egg and combine it with the buttermilk.

Now take the butter chunks out of the fridge and put them into the dry mix a few at a time. You want to try to completely coat the butter pieces with the flour mix. At this point, put both hands into the bowl and roll the flour and butter between your thumbs and fingers, letting the contents drop back into the bowl each time. Keep the mixture moving through your hands with minimal pressure and contact. The finished batter should have a gravelly texture—shot through with uneven-sized pebbles of butter.

Next, gradually cut the buttermilk-egg mixture through the butter-flour mixture with a fork (or your fingers—which is better) until you reach a consistency that allows you to make two equal-sized balls of dough. Sooner is better than later—you don't want to overwork this dough!

Gently flatten these balls into disks approximately 6 inches in diameter. Don't knead the dough! Cut the disks into 4 triangular sections as though you were cutting four slices of pizza out of each disk.

Place the 8 triangles on an ungreased cookie sheet. Beat the other egg and brush it over the scones. Bake in the oven for about 20 minutes, until they are golden brown. Serve warm with butter, honey, or jam. They are also very good without anything else at all.

FOR A VARIATION OF THIS RECIPE TRY
SCONES WITH DRIED FRUIT.

Follow the preceding recipe for scones, but take out 2 tablespoons of the sugar. Add 2 tablespoons each of dried blueberries, dried cranberries, and golden raisins. Blend these into the pebbled butter-sugar-flour with your fingers, before you add the egg-buttermilk mixture. Continue with the instructions for my scones.

These scones stand on their own: They are light and delicious and require no assistance from jam or honey.

Pineapple Scones

Makes 8 scones

Summer scones, summer scones, sum, sum, summer scones . . . anyway, these scones are great in the summertime.

4 tablespoons (¼ cup, or ½ stick) cold butter
2 cups all-purpose flour
¼ cup sugar, less 2 tablespoons
½ teaspoon cinnamon
4 teaspoon salt
1 tablespoon baking powder
¼ teaspoon baking soda
2 eggs (1 for brushing)
½ cup buttermilk
1 cup pineapple, cubed to about ½ inch

Preheat the oven to 350 degrees.

Cut the butter into small (¼-inch) chunks and return it to the refrigerator.

In a large bowl, combine all the dry ingredients: flour, sugar, cinnamon, salt, baking powder, and baking soda. Beat 1 egg in your mixing cup and combine it with the buttermilk.

Retrieve the butter chunks from the fridge and add them to the flour mixture, keeping them separated, if possible, when you coat them in the dry ingredients. Finger through the mixture, rolling the butter-flour-sugar through your thumbs and fingers. Continue until you get to a gravelly texture with uneven-sized pebbles of butter. Keep pulling your hands up and out of the dough so the warmth of your hands doesn't melt the butter. (Warmhearted people make good bakers because they have cold hands—ha!)

Now add the buttermilk mixture, pineapple, and raisins, combing it through with your hands just long enough to be able to create two equal-sized balls of dough.

Flatten the balls into 2 disks about 6 inches in diameter. Cut each disk into 4 slices and place the 8 triangles on an ungreased cookie sheet. Beat the other egg and brush it on the scones. Bake for 20 minutes, until they are golden brown. (When a scone is perfectly done, it will have a hollow sound when you tap on the bottom. Don't burn yourself!)

Apple Scones

Makes 8 scones

*T*his one is good all year long, but better in the fall, cliff-side or no, wherever you can find Granny Smith apples. (I have to amend the preceding: I don't make apple scones in June—my purveyor tells me that's the month the Grannies have been sitting too long in the warehouse.)

4 tablespoons (¼ cup, or ½ stick) cold butter
1½ cups all-purpose flour
½ cup wheat germ
¼ cup sugar
½ teaspoon cinnamon
1 tablespoon baking powder
¼ teaspoon baking soda
2 eggs (1 for glazing)
½ cup buttermilk
1 Granny Smith apple (peeled and cut into ½-inch cubes, about 1 cup)

Preheat the oven to 350 degrees.

Cut the butter into small (¼-inch) chunks, rewrap it in the paper, and return it to the refrigerator.

Review the "master" scone recipe on page 115.

Combine the dry ingredients. Beat 1 egg and combine it with the buttermilk. Thread the butter through the dry ingredients with thumbs and fingers, getting it to a gravelly texture.

Comb the buttermilk-egg mixture into the butter-flour "gravel," then add the apple cubes, blending through the batter just enough to be able to make two equal-sized balls.

Flatten the balls to 2 disks 5 to 6 inches in diameter. Now "pizza-slice" each disk into 4 sections. Put the scones on an ungreased cookie sheet. Beat the second egg and brush it on the scones as a glaze.

Bake for 20 minutes, until golden brown.

Savory Scones

Makes 8 scones

The term savory in gastronomic lingo refers to foods that are spiced or seasoned as opposed to sweet. So if you're in an unsweet kind of mood and have a yen for something with a little fire in it, these may be just the scones for you. They're great with a glass of full-bodied red wine such as a Rhône or even a Beaujolais Village.

1 dried chipotle pepper sliced in half (or canned
    equivalent)
¼ cup milk
8 tablespoons cold butter (½ cup or 1 stick)
⅛ teaspoon dry mustard
⅛ teaspoon paprika
⅛ teaspoon black pepper
⅛ teaspoon red pepper flakes (if not using the chipotle)
1 teaspoon vegetable oil
4 tablespoons raw pumpkin seeds
2 cups plus 3 tablespoons all-purpose flour
1½ teaspoons sugar
¼ teaspoon salt
1 tablespoon baking powder
¼ teaspoon baking soda
2 eggs (1 for glazing)
½ cup buttermilk
½ cup grated sharp cheddar cheese (loosely packed for
    measurement)

Preheat the oven to 350 degrees.

Put the halved chipotle together with the ¼ cup milk in a small pot and bring to a scald over high heat. (In scalding you bring the milk to a point just below boiling. Also, I leave in some of the seeds of the chipotle—they are the hottest part of the pepper. If you prefer less fire, you can remove them.) Immediately reduce the heat, simmer for 10 minutes, and remove from the heat.

Cut the butter into small (¼-inch) pieces and return it to the refrigerator.

Put all of the spices (and red pepper flakes if using instead of chipotle) except the salt with the vegetable oil in a frying pan and heat until sizzling. Then put in the pumpkin seeds. Cook for 7 minutes, shaking the pan now and then to keep the seeds moving around. They will get toasty brown and give off a nutty aroma when done.

In a large bowl mix together the flour, sugar, salt, baking powder, and baking soda. Take the butter out of the fridge and try your best to coat each piece with the flour mixture before you begin to run it through your thumbs and fingers. You want a gravelly mixture with little pieces of butter in it (see Carrie's Scones, p. 115).

Now strain the chipotle from the milk. Beat 1 of the eggs and mix the milk, egg, and buttermilk together.

With a fork, comb the spicy pumpkin seeds through the butter-flour mixture. Next, add the milk-egg mixture and blend everything together. Finally, work the grated cheddar in.

Make 2 balls of equal size with your dough and flatten them into disks 5 to 6 inches in diameter. Cut these "pies" into a total of 8 slices and place them on an ungreased cookie sheet. Beat the remaining egg and add a few drops of water to it, then brush it over the scones to glaze.

Bake in the oven for about 20 minutes.

These are great with some slices of ham or any smoked meat. For a sweet and savory experience, try them with some Strawberry Jam (p. 154).

Eggless Scones with Raisins and Mint

Makes 8 scones

*T*he recipe for these scones came about through a collaboration with one of my great friends, who is also an aficionado of scones. He has always loved mine, and when he moved to Michigan, he would have boxes of them flown to him there. While he was away in Michigan, he discovered that he was allergic to eggs, and he knew that scones are made with eggs. He called in great distress and we started to research.

I had my moment of inspiration while reading the label on a jar of Mott's Apple Sauce, and it was his idea to use jelly for a glaze. My friend has since moved back to NYC, and together we made these scones in my kitchen one afternoon.

12 tablespoons (¾ cup, 1½ sticks) cold butter
2 cups all-purpose flour
2 tablespoons sugar
½ teaspoon salt
1 tablespoon baking powder
¼ teaspoon baking soda
¼ cup golden raisins
1 tablespoon chiffonade mint leaves ("chiffonade" means
    cut into thin strips)
5 tablespoons applesauce
½ cup plain, whole-milk yogurt
3 tablespoons mint jelly plus 1 tablespoon water warmed
    together for glaze

Note: The applesauce functions as a substitute for 1 egg in this recipe. If you're allergic to applesauce (!), there are egg substitutes sold in health food stores.

Preheat the oven to 350 degrees.

Cut the butter into small chunks (about ¼ inch square) and return to the refrigerator.

Combine the flour, sugar, salt, baking powder, and baking soda in a large bowl. Retrieve the butter and add it, piece by piece, to the flour mixture, coating each chunk. That done, begin rolling the butter and the flour mixture together, pushing with your thumb over your fingers to create the gravelly dry dough. Remember to keep lifting your hands to let the dough fall back into the bowl—you don't want the warmth of your hands to melt the butter.

Put the raisins and mint leaves into the mixture and just move them around enough to coat them with dough. Now add the applesauce and yogurt and continue the blending action with your hands until it is incorporated into the dough.

Divide the dough in half and make 2 balls. Flatten the balls into 2 pielike disks and cut them into a total of 8 slices. Place the scones on a nonstick cookie sheet or line your sheet with parchment paper. Brush the dissolved mint jelly over the scones to glaze. Bake for 20 to 25 minutes. These scones will not get as golden brown as the others. Check with a fork for dry tines as the done signal.

These eggless scones are a little lighter and chewier than the eggy ones, and they're very tasty.

Eggless, Wheatless, Sugarless Scones with Maple Whipped Cream

Makes 8 scones

I think it was Stanislavski who said, "Less is more." If you look at it that way, these scones have a lot going for them.

Since they have no egg or wheat gluten to hold them together, they are quite delicate to handle. Don't try to pile them on top of each other after you take them out of the oven. I serve these scones with Maple Whipped Cream.

½ **cup macadamia nuts, chopped and toasted**
12 **tablespoons (¾ cup, 1½ sticks) cold butter**

2 cups white spelt flour
1 tablespoon baking powder
½ teaspoon salt
¼ teaspoon ground nutmeg
½ teaspoon ground cardamom
⅛ teaspoon ground cloves
¼ cup strong coffee (brewed)
¼ cup heavy cream
2 tablespoons molasses
4 tablespoons applesauce (or egg substitute equivalent
  to 1 egg)

Preheat the oven to 350 degrees. Spread the macadamias on a cookie sheet, and when the oven is hot, toast the nuts for 10 minutes, moving them around a couple of times. Let the nuts cool when done.

Cut the butter into small chunks (about ¼ inch square) and return to refrigerator until called for.

In a large bowl combine the spelt flour, baking powder, salt, nutmeg, cardamom, and cloves. Now take the butter and coat each chunk with the flour mixture before using your hands to work it into a gravelly dough. See Carrie's Scones for technique page 115.

Work the cooled macadamia nuts into the dough just enough to coat them.

In another bowl mix the coffee, cream, molasses, and applesauce together. Now comb this mixture with your fingers through the flour mixture just enough to combine.

Divide the dough in half, making 2 balls. Flatten the balls into big pie-shaped disks, then slice each pie to create a total of 8 slices. Put the scones on an ungreased cookie sheet and bake in the oven for 25 to 30 minutes. Use a toothpick to check for doneness, as a fork may break them.

Take them out of the oven carefully and don't pile them on top of each other when transferring from the cookie sheet. Serve with Maple Whipped Cream.

Note: I'm not quite truthful in calling these "sugarless," since they do contain molasses, and of course maple syrup is sweet, too.

Maple Whipped Cream

¾ cup heavy cream
½ teaspoon pure vanilla extract
1 tablespoon maple syrup

Put the heavy cream, vanilla, and maple syrup into a dry, cool bowl and whip until the cream holds a soft peak. That's it. Dollop it on the scones, or on top of your coffee, or both.

BISCUITS

I frankly have no apotheosis to relate when it comes to biscuits. I never encountered a biscuit, as we know it in the States, during my sixteen years of growing up in Europe. And I suppose, for the English, the scone is the closest thing to a biscuit. To compound the confusion, the English call cookies biscuits (and underwear pants, sweaters jumpers, pants trousers . . .).

I think I had biscuits in America when I came here in the summer to visit my grandparents, but they evidentally didn't make any impression on me. The biscuits I make at Good Enough to Eat came from Ann, who was my partner when the restaurant first opened. They came to her from a friend's mother, from an "old Southern family recipe."

Anyway, Ann's friend's mom's Southern family biscuits were the perfect sidekick for our egg dishes, and with Strawberry Butter they do elicit numinous moans from our customers.

Good Enough to Eat Biscuits with Strawberry Butter

Makes 24 to 26 biscuits

1 cup vegetable shortening plus a little more for
  greasing the pan
4½ teaspoons dry yeast (2 packets less ½ teaspoon)
2 tablespoons sugar plus a pinch for the yeast
2 tablespoons warm water
5 cups all-purpose flour plus extra for flouring
1 teaspoon baking soda
2 tablespoons baking powder
1 teaspoon salt
2 cups buttermilk
2 tablespoons melted butter for brushing

Note: Although you certainly can make this recipe without
one, I do recommend that you use a standing electric mixer
with at least a 10-cup bowl and use the paddle attachment
(not a bread hook).

Preheat the oven to 350 degrees. Lightly grease the baking
sheet(s) with some vegetable shortening.

Dissolve the yeast with a pinch of sugar in the warm water
and let it stand for 3 to 5 minutes. It will foam up a bit.

In the mixer bowl combine the 5 cups flour, baking soda,
baking powder, salt, and sugar. Use a very slow speed for all
mixing, particularly for this first step, or you'll have flour all
over the kitchen—and make sure you stop the mixer before
you add ingredients.

Add the shortening and blend it in until you reach a
coarse, gravelly texture with little bits of shortening
throughout the flour mix. Pour in the yeast and blend in for
a few seconds. Now add the buttermilk and mix in until you
see the dough come up around the paddle—this will happen
pretty quickly—and stop.

Lift the dough out of the mixer bowl and place it on a

clean, dry board. Push the dough down with your fingertips until it is 1 to 1¼ inches thick. Using a 2-inch biscuit cutter, push the cutter at an angle against the near edge of the dough, then roll it away from you and down into the dough to cut the first biscuit. With a twist of the wrist lift the first biscuit out and place it on the greased baking sheet.

There will be little hooks in the dough from cutting the first biscuit. Push the cutter into one of those hooks, absorbing it into the second biscuit, then roll down to cut, and use a little twist to lift out. Place the second biscuit on the baking sheet right up against the first one. Proceed this way, cutting biscuits and packing them on the baking sheet(s), until you're out of dough.

Bake in the oven for about 20 minutes, or until the biscuits are slightly golden. Take them out of the oven and brush the tops with melted butter.

Serve the biscuits warm with Strawberry Butter (recipe follows).

Note: We bake biscuits and scones every morning at the restaurant. However, at home you can store any extra biscuits in the freezer for future use, and since their preparation is time-consuming, I recommend that you do so. Reheat right out of the freezer in a 200-degree oven for 15 minutes.

Strawberry Butter

Makes 1¼ cups

1 cup (2 sticks) soft butter
3 ounces (4 tablespoons) Strawberry Jam (p. 154)

Beat the butter in the food processor until it is white. Add the jam and beat until smooth.

Drop Biscuits

Makes 12 biscuits

This is a quick and easy recipe for biscuits that makes a practical amount for a small family. The biscuits are light and flaky and don't require yeast. You also don't need to use a mixer, so cleaning up is easier.

Mrs. White, who is my mother's best friend, passed the recipe on to me from a method used by her mother, who celebrated her 106th birthday on August 13, 2000, which, coincidentally, was Good Enough to Eat's nineteenth anniversary. Happy Birthday to us both!

1 tablespoon cornmeal (for the baking sheet)
1 cup all-purpose flour
2 teaspoons baking powder
⅛ teaspoon salt
3 tablespoons vegetable shortening (I use Crisco)
7 tablespoons milk

Preheat the oven to 425 degrees. Dust the baking sheet with cornmeal.

Combine the flour, baking powder, and salt in a large bowl. Now incorporate the shortening into the flour mixture, using the same technique as described in the recipe for Good Enough to Eat Biscuits. The batter should be coarse with bits of shortening. Lastly, incorporate the milk, working it through the batter with your fingers. The resulting batter should have the consistency of cooked oatmeal.

With a teaspoon, put little dumpling heaps of the batter onto the prepared baking sheet, pushing the batter off the spoon with your finger. Bake in the oven for 10 to 12 minutes, until golden brown. If you like, you can brush some melted butter over the biscuits when they come out of the oven.

Note: You could double the size of the biscuits and make strawberry shortcake (or short biscuits!) with some strawberries and whipped cream.

Sweet Potato Biscuits

Makes about 15 biscuits

These are really good if you like sweet potatoes. I made them at home, and my husband, Bill, ate four right out of the oven with butter before I chased him out of the kitchen. I had made the biscuits to go with a pork chop dinner, and he finished that with two more biscuits.

2 medium sweet potatoes, peeled and cut up for boiling
    (2 cups)
8 tablespoons (½ cup, 1 stick) cold butter (reserve one
    tablespoon for brushing)
½ teaspoon salt
⅛ teaspoon black pepper
⅛ teaspoon red pepper flakes
2 tablespoons orange juice
2 tablespoons milk
2 cups all-purpose flour
1 tablespoon baking powder
¼ teaspoon baking soda
2 tablespoons sugar

Peel the sweet potatoes and cut them up for boiling. Boil until tender, drain, and mash. Push the mashed potatoes to one side of the pot, and with the handle of a wooden serving spoon make holes in the potato to let the steam escape. On the other side of the pot, put one tablespoon of butter with the salt, pepper, and red pepper flakes. Return to medium heat and simmer for 5 minutes. Stir in the orange juice and cook for another 2 minutes. Remove the pot from the heat, stir in the milk, and put in a bowl to cool. Note that since the sweet potatoes need to be cool, you should prepare them well in advance of making the biscuits.

In a large bowl, combine the flour, baking powder, baking soda, and sugar. Cut 6 tablespoons of butter into small pieces and coat each piece in the flour. Now run the butter and flour through your thumbs and fingers to create the coarse biscuit dough.

Mix in the cooled sweet potatoes and knead on a lightly floured board just enough to combine. Now push the dough out into a pancake shape about ½ inch thick.

Using a 2-inch biscuit cutter and following the technique for using it (described on page 126), cut your biscuits and place them on a lightly greased or nonstick baking sheet just touching each other. Bake for 20 to 25 minutes, until golden. Brush with some melted butter when done, and hide them from the family until dinnertime.

English Muffins

Makes 10 muffins

These are "really quite lovely," as my English chum Amanda would say. They are yeasty and a little heavier than the store-boughts. English muffins are really more of a bread than a muffin and are quite at their loveliest right after they are baked, but wrapped, they will keep quite nicely in the refrigerator.

Make these with a standing mixer using the dough hook; and you will need an English muffin cutter, which happens to be almost the exact dimensions of a 12-ounce can of tunafish—hint! hint! Remove the top and bottom of the can and soak in lemon juice, water, and baking soda (combined) to get out the smell.

2½ teaspoons dry yeast (1 packet)
½ cup warm water
2 teaspoons sugar
½ cup plus 2 tablespoons milk
1 teaspoon salt
4 tablespoons (¼ cup, ½ stick) soft butter
3 cups all-purpose flour
2 tablespoons cornmeal

Put the yeast into 2 tablespoons of the warm (105 to 115 degrees) water with a pinch of the sugar and let it sit. (If the yeast is alive, as it should be, it will "eat" the sugar and the reaction will cause the mixture to foam up a bit. If there has been no reaction, your yeast is dead and you have to try again. The water has to be warm, not hot.)

Scald the milk (heat it to just below boiling) and add the rest of the water and sugar and the salt. Cut up the butter and put the pieces into the milk mixture.

Put the flour into the mixer bowl and add the milk-butter mixture. Mix with the dough hook to combine. Now add the yeast and combine until the dough comes up around the dough hook.

Remove the dough from the mixer bowl and place it in another clean bowl that you have greased with a little butter. Let the dough sit on the countertop near the stove (a warm place) and rise for 30 minutes. Sprinkle some cornmeal on your board or countertop, put the dough on the board, and knock it down, pushing out the air. Push the dough out with your fingertips until it is uniformly 1 inch thick.

Using your English muffin cutter (or your tuna can), cut out 10 muffins and place them on a baking sheet dusted with cornmeal. (See cutter technique on p. 126). Put the muffins back in their warm spot and let them rise again for at least 1 hour.

Preheat the griddle to medium-low.

Put the muffins on the hot griddle and cook them about 7½ minutes on each side, until pale gold in color.

After they've cooked, you can cut them in half to toast and serve with butter and honey, with cream cheese and jam, or under a poached egg.

Coffee Cake, Doughnuts, and Danish

You have done your apprenticeship in baking in the previous chapters on breads, muffins, and biscuits. This chapter brings us to graduate school, combining earlier techniques and increasing the levels of intricacy and finesse needed for success.

I have arranged the sections in order of difficulty as I perceive them to be, beginning with coffee cake and cinnamon buns, followed by doughnuts, and ending with Danish pastry. I have appended a recipe for a sweet turnover to complement the savories in earlier chapters and to underscore the versatility of puff pastry. We conclude with the airy somethings called popovers.

COFFEE CAKE

Sour Cream Coffee Cake with Crumb Topping

Makes a 9-inch cake, about 12 slices

*T*his recipe had its genesis in one of those bed-and-breakfast villages in eastern Massachusetts that Bill and I visited about twenty years ago before we were married. Like other epiphanies I have experienced in my obsessive career with food, I felt I had found the perfect coffee cake. Well, it was nearly perfect—and now it is!

There are three stages of preparation, given in order. If there's one "secret," it's the vanilla bath. If there's one critical technique, it's the way you fold or pulse in the flour.

Preheat the oven to 350 degrees.

For the streusel:

3 tablespoons cold butter
½ cup packed dark brown sugar
1½ teaspoons cinnamon
½ cup coarsely chopped walnuts

Cut the butter into little pieces and mix together with the other ingredients until you reach a gravelly consistency. Put in the refrigerator to keep the butter from melting until ready to use.

For the cake:

1½ sticks (12 tablespoons) soft butter
1¼ cups sugar
3 eggs
1 teaspoon pure vanilla extract (for cake) plus 2
    tablespoons (for bath)
2½ cups all-purpose flour
2 teaspoons baking powder
1 teaspoon baking soda
½ teaspoon salt
1½ cups sour cream

Grease a 9-inch tube pan with some butter (not from ingredients), and flour it, banging out the excess.

Using a standing mixer or a food processor, beat the butter and sugar together thoroughly until white. Stop the processor. Using a rubber spatula, scrape down any mix that has climbed the sides of the bowl. Break the eggs into a measuring cup and stir together with the 1 teaspoon of vanilla. Add this to the processor and beat together at high speed until incorporated. Stop the processor and scrape down. If the mixture has a curdled appearance, that's good.

Combine the flour with the baking powder, baking soda, and salt. Make sure there are no unmixed lumps of any of the rising elements. Put one-third of the flour into the processor and pulse for 2 to 3 seconds. Scrape down. Add half of the sour cream; pulse for 2 to 3 seconds. Scrape down. Continue: one-third flour, pulse, scrape down; one-half sour cream, pulse, scrape down; one-third flour, pulse, scrape down; and so on. Make sure everything is incorporated—pulse again if necessary. Remember to stop the processor each time while scraping down and adding ingredients.

Put half of the cake batter into your tube pan. Drop the streusel evenly over the top, and bang down the pan to settle. Now add the rest of the cake batter. Drizzle the 2 tablespoons of vanilla over the top of the batter (the "bath").

Put into the oven to bake for 50 to 60 minutes. At the 30-minute point you will put on the crumb topping.

Crumb Topping

1 cup all-purpose flour
¼ teaspoon salt
2 tablespoons sugar
½ teaspoon baking powder
7 tablespoons chilled, cut-up butter

In a bowl at room temperature, mix the flour, salt, sugar, and baking powder. Mix the butter into the dry mix as described in the recipe for Carrie's Scones (p. 115), with minimal touching of the butter, ending up with a coarse, gravel-like mixture. After the cake has been in the oven for 30 minutes, sprinkle the topping onto the coffee cake. Don't squeeze or press the topping down.

The coffee cake will be done after about 25 more minutes in the oven. Test with a slender, long-bladed knife: After inserting in the middle, it should come out dry.

Let the cake cool for 15 minutes before removing from pan and slicing to serve.

VARIATIONS

1. The streusel recipe can be doubled and put on top of the cake batter (as well as in the middle) at the beginning of the baking time.

2. Cut-up pieces of peaches, pears, strawberries, or apples, or whole blueberries or cherries, can be incorporated into the batter after the final stage of blending. Skip the streusel in the middle and top the cake with either streusel or Crumb Topping. This is the variation of coffee cake that we serve at the restaurant during the summer. The staff's favorite is the blueberry.

Sour Cream Coffee Cake is so popular with our customers that it is in the pastry case breakfast, lunch, and dinner.

Orange-Apricot-Pecan Coffee Cake

Makes 1 ten-inch coffee cake

This is a coffee cake designed to remind me of one I had at Schrafft's when my grandmother would take me there as a kid. I doubt if anyone under forty will remember Schrafft's. It was on the East Side and was the sort of place that grandmothers would take their grandchildren—all dressed up, of course—for ice cream and cake.

The dough for this coffee cake is more like a bread dough: It uses yeast and requires kneading, rising, rolling . . . it is more pastry than cake. I'm afraid I've jumped you right into graduate school!

I use a standing electric mixer with the paddle attachment and a piping bag with a number 230 tip for this recipe.

1 packet dry yeast
¼ cup warm water (110 degrees)
Pinch sugar
3 cups all-purpose flour plus 2 tablespoons for flouring
1 teaspoon salt
2 tablespoons sugar
½ teaspoon baking soda
1 orange
¼ cup sour cream
½ cup plus 2 tablespoons scalded milk
2 eggs (white of 1 reserved for icing)
3 tablespoons butter plus 1 tablespoon for rising bowl
3 tablespoons cream cheese
¾ cup toasted pecan halves
¾ cup slivered dried apricots
3 tablespoons apricot or peach jam
1 to 1¼ cups confectioners' sugar

Put the yeast into the warm water with the pinch of sugar and let sit for 5 to 7 minutes in a warm spot for the sponge.

At low speed combine in the mixer the 3 cups of flour, salt, sugar, and baking soda. Zest the orange and save the rest. Combine two-thirds of the zest with the sour cream and scalded milk. Whisk 1 whole egg and 1 yolk in a separate bowl.

Add the 3 tablespoons of butter and cream cheese in small pieces to the mixer and combine until mixture is crumbly. (As a general rule, stop the mixer and scrape down the sides before every addition.) Add the eggs and beat for a few seconds. Add the milk mixture and beat a few seconds. Now add the yeast sponge and beat until the dough comes up around the paddle and takes on a silky appearance.

Remove to the board. Flour the board only if the dough sticks. Knead a few times and place in a large glass bowl greased with the 1 tablespoon of butter. Roll the dough to coat it, cover with a clean dish towel, and place in a warm spot to rise for 1 to 1½ hours, until doubled.

In the meantime, the pecans can be toasted, if they're not already, by spreading on a baking sheet and putting in a 350-degree oven for 10 minutes. The apricots should be put into enough boiling water to cover, with a slice of the zested orange. Let the water return to a boil, then turn off the heat and let the pot sit, covered, for 10 minutes. Drain the water and pat the apricots dry. Both apricots and pecans should be cool before using.

Bring the dough back to the board and cut it in half. Roll each piece into a rectangle approximately 4 x 12 inches. Reserve ¼ cup of the pecans and distribute the rest along with the apricots over the surface of your two rectangles of dough. Roll closed along the long side as tightly as you can without tearing the dough and pinch the long edge of the "snakes" into the dough surface to close.

(This last bit and what follows will test your mettle—you do not want to tear the dough; if you do, you won't receive your master's degree!)

Now roll the two snakes very carefully until they are about 18 inches long. Pinch the ends together. Twine the snakes together—think herpetological love—and then form a ring about 8 inches across. (If you've gotten this far without mishap, I would discard the measuring tape.) Pinch the ends together, cover the ring, and let it rise for another ½ hour.

Preheat the oven to 350 degrees. You might want to do this earlier if the temperature in the kitchen is below 65 degrees, to help the dough rise.

For the glaze: Squeeze the juice from the zested orange and combine 1 tablespoon of the juice with 3 tablespoons apricot jam in a small pot. Simmer and stir until melted and mixed— about 10 minutes.

Back to the dough: Place the risen ring on a nonstick sheet or on parchment paper on a cookie sheet. Brush on the apricot glaze lavishly. Bake for 30 to 35 minutes, until golden brown. It should have a slightly hollow sound when tapped. Let it cool for 15 to 20 minutes before icing.

For the icing: Combine 2 tablespoons of egg white with the remaining third of orange zest, 1 tablespoon of the orange juice, and a generous cup of sifted confectioners' sugar. Mix well until thick enough to put in the piping bag. Arrange the rest of the pecans on the top of the cake, and apply the icing as though you were Jackson Pollack. That's it. Did you graduate?

Perfect Cinnamon Buns

Makes 14 buns

I've literally spent years working on this recipe. Cinnamon buns are a basic, familiar pastry, and like other breakfast standards, I've been obsessed with perfecting them. It has been a nerve-racking obsession, and despite calling them perfect, I'm going to make another batch tonight, just to make sure.

Although this is a yeasted dough, it should be handled more like a muffin batter—don't overwork it! It comes together fast, and once it does, let it be, let it be, let it be . . . there will be an answer. . . .

You need a standing electric mixer fitted with the paddle attachment and a 9-inch cake pan.

For the dough:

1 cup milk
4 tablespoons sugar
1 packet dry yeast
3½ to 4 cups all-purpose flour
1½ teaspoons salt
¼ teaspoon baking soda
1 egg
1 teaspoon pure vanilla extract
Zest of ½ lemon
¼ cup sour cream
Butter for rising bowl, pan, and brushing

For the filling:

½ stick (4 tablespoons) butter
½ cup dark brown sugar
2 teaspoons cinnamon

For the icing:

1 cup confectioners' sugar
⅓ cup water or milk

To make the dough, combine the milk and 1 tablespoon of the sugar in a saucepan. Simmer and stir until the sugar is dissolved. Let the milk cool to 105 to 115 degrees. To ½ cup of the milk add the yeast, stir gently, and let sit for 3 to 5 minutes.

In a large bowl combine 3½ cups of flour with the rest of the sugar, the salt, and the baking soda. In a small bowl or measuring cup beat the egg together with the vanilla, lemon zest, and sour cream.

Put one-third of the flour mix into the bowl of the mixer and add the yeast sponge. Beat just enough to combine. Add the egg mixture and beat to combine. Add one-third more flour and combine. Add the remaining milk and combine. Add remaining flour to combine. (Remember to stop the mixer and scrape down the sides of the mixer bowl before each added ingredient.)

You are looking for the dough to be silky and resilient to the touch. If it is a little sticky when you remove it to the board, dust with a little flour and knead—as little flour and handling as possible. Place the dough in a large glass or ceramic bowl with about 1 teaspoon of melted or very soft butter, coat the dough, and cover with a clean dish towel to rise in a warm place (75 degrees) for about 1 hour, or until doubled in size.

To make the filling, use your hands to combine in a small bowl the butter, brown sugar, and cinnamon, trying to disperse little bits of solid butter throughout.

Once the dough has doubled, knock it down to let the air out; knead a little to return the dough to its silky texture. Roll the dough out into a rectangle 4 x 15 inches. Spread the filling evenly over the dough, just avoiding the far edge. Now roll the dough into a cylinder along the long edge, tucking with the fingertips to make it as tight as possible without tearing it. Seal the cylinder by pinching the far edge into the surface of the dough.

Turn the cylinder seam side down and cut 14 slices about 1 inch thick. Arrange the slices, touching, in a 9-inch cake pan that has been buttered on the sides and bottom. Cover with a clean dish towel and set in a warm place to rise for about ½ hour. The buns will fill the pan.

Preheat the oven to 350 degrees. Once the buns have risen, brush them with a little melted butter and bake for 20 to 25 minutes, until a light golden brown.

Make the icing by dissolving the confectioners' sugar in the water or milk. When the buns are done, flip them upside down onto a plate. Turn the cake pan upside down and flip the buns right side up onto it. Drizzle the icing onto the buns while they're still hot so that it dribbles a little down the sides. Perfect!

DOUGHNUTS

Churros, piscarones, bombolinis, beignets, donuts—by any name they're fried, sugary dough. Having been brought up in Europe, I have always thought of the doughnut as being peculiarly American. However, Amanda Hesser, in an article for the *New York Times* (October 18, 2000), cites: "It is possible, David A. Taylor wrote in a 1998 article in *Smithsonian* magazine, that it (the doughnut) descended from a Dutch pastry called oly-koeks, or 'oily cakes.' The name dough-nuts, he wrote, came later, from Elizabeth Gregory, a New England home cook in the mid-nineteenth century, who made fried dough filled with nuts (dough-nuts) and lemon rind for her son, who later took credit for the hole."

Interesting!

Quick Doughnuts

Makes 6 to 9 doughnuts

This doughnut is close to cake in texture, but the dry and liquid ingredients are combined in the same one-third, one-half, one-third, one-half, one-third sequence as described on page 133. It seems overly fractionalized, but it works. I discovered it when working on my "perfect" chocolate cake. See my first book (Good Enough to Eat: Bountiful Home Cooking, Simon & Schuster, 1987) *for that recipe—some people actually do have cake for breakfast.*

The critical part of the doughnut recipes is keeping the oil at a constant 375 degrees. I have the best luck with a heavy, commercial-grade aluminum pot. You could also use a Dutch oven of cast iron. Besides a good pot, you will need a long-handled spoon with a wire basket to lift the doughnuts in and out of the oil, a doughnut cutter, and a thermometer suitable for checking the temperature of the hot oil (ask at a kitchen supply store).

1 quart vegetable oil (you need at least 3 inches of oil in
   the pot for the frying—I use canola oil)
2½ cups all-purpose flour
1 teaspoon baking powder
½ teaspoon salt
¼ teaspoon nutmeg
¼ teaspoon ground cloves
½ teaspoon cinnamon
2 eggs
½ cup sugar
3 tablespoons melted butter
1 tablespoon lemon juice
¼ cup milk
Cinnamon-sugar (1 tablespoon cinnamon to 4 tablespoons
   sugar), *or*
Powdered sugar to roll the doughnuts in

Heat 3 inches of vegetable oil in a heavy pot over medium heat. You want to bring the oil to about 320 degrees before you're ready to cook. Put the thermometer in to check. You don't want the oil to smoke!

Sift together into a large bowl the flour, baking powder, salt, nutmeg, cloves, and cinnamon. In a separate bowl, beat the eggs and the sugar together until light, then combine with the butter, lemon juice, and milk.

Add one-third of the flour to the bowl of a standing mixer equipped with a paddle. Add one-half of the liquid mixture and beat enough to combine. Stop the mixer, scrape down the sides, and add one-third more flour. Beat to combine. Stop. Repeat scraping. Add remaining liquid. Beat to combine. Stop. Scrape. Combine remaining flour.

Remove the dough to the board. The dough will be loose, but flour it only if it sticks. Roll the dough out to ½ inch thickness. Using the doughnut cutter, cut in a rolling movement in from the edge of the dough; reserve the holes for cooking. Push the two "hooks" into the dough and proceed to cut the next doughnut, and so on.

Raise the heat to bring the oil to 375. You can check to see if the oil is hot enough by dropping a little chunk of white bread in. If the bread immediately bobs to the surface and lightly browns, you're ready for the doughnuts.

Ease the donuts into the oil. They shouldn't be crowded—2 or 3 at a time, depending on the size of your pot. Cook 3 to 4 minutes on the first side; use the wire spoon to turn and cook 2 to 3 minutes on the second side. Remove to drain on some paper towels or cardboard egg cartons (which are perfect for this). If the temperature drops during cooking, get it back up to 375 before you put in the next doughnuts. Be very careful not to rinse your wire spoon or put anything with any water on it into the oil—it will splatter!

Cook the holes in the same way. They will take less time, but like the doughnuts, they will get a rich golden brown when done. And be sure to take full "credit" for them!

Roll the doughnuts while they are still warm in some cinnamon-sugar or powdered sugar if you like. If you burn a couple a little bit, roll them in some sugar anyway. My husband loved them.

Note: Canola oil is expensive. I strain it and save it for two more subsequent deep fryings. To tell you the unchic truth, Crisco is cheaper and will work just as well.

Baked Jelly Doughnuts

Makes 6 or 7 doughnuts

I've never met a kid who didn't like jelly doughnuts. Maybe it's the sweet squish that comes with biting into them. Then, of course, you always have to lick around your lips a lot. You'll need a piping bag and a number 230 tip to inject the jelly. I think the doughnut stands usually put a cherry-flavored jelly in theirs, but you can use your own favorite. Try elderberry; it's quite nice.

1½ teaspoons dry yeast
¼ cup warm water
2 tablespoons plus a pinch of sugar
¼ cup plus 1 tablespoon scalded milk
¾ teaspoon salt
1⅔ cups all-purpose flour
3 tablespoons cold butter, cut in small pieces, plus 1
    tablespoon melted butter (for brushing)
1 egg
½ cup jelly
2 tablespoons powdered sugar

Preheat the oven to 450 degrees. Flour a baking sheet.

Stir the yeast into the warm water with a pinch of sugar. Set it in a warm place for 3 to 5 minutes to develop the sponge.

Scald the milk. You do this to have the milk close to the same temperature as the warm water when things are combined. As with the water, it should be warm to the wrist, like the milk for a baby's bottle.

Combine the salt and the flour in a large bowl, then add the pieces of butter, combining until the mixture has a crumbly texture, containing bits of butter.

Beat the egg together with the milk.

Put half of the flour into the bowl of a standing mixer

fitted with the paddle. Stir the yeast together with the milk-egg mixture and add half of it to the mixer. Beat to combine. Add the rest of the flour. Beat to combine. Finish by adding the rest of the liquid, scraping down the sides, and beating until the dough comes together.

Flour your rolling board if the dough is sticky, and roll the dough out to ¾ inch thickness. Using a 3-inch cookie cutter, cut out by starting from the outside edge and cutting into the dough with a rolling movement. Place the doughnut on the floured baking sheet. Push in the "hooks" with the cutter and cut out the second doughnut, and so on, lightly flouring the cutter if the dough is sticking.

Cover the baking sheet with a clean dish towel and put the doughnuts in a warm place to rise until doubled—45 minutes to 1 hour.

Bake for about 15 minutes or until a light, golden brown. When done, remove from the oven and let the doughnuts cool for 10 minutes. With the jelly in the piping bag, insert the nozzle into the side of the doughnuts and squirt in about 1 tablespoon of jelly. Brush the doughnuts with some melted butter and dust with powdered sugar. Call the kids!

Chocolate Doughnuts

Makes 8

My oldest boy, Bucko, pronounced these doughnuts "the best ever." Like me, he loves chocolate.

We're back to the frying oil here, so you'll need the thermometer, the big, heavy pot, lots of oil, and the long-handled wire basket spoon.

1 quart vegetable oil (or enough to fill frying pot at least
   3 inches deep)
½ cup packed dark brown sugar
2 tablespoons butter
2 cups all-purpose flour plus 3 tablespoons for board and
   cutter
½ teaspoon salt
2½ teaspoons baking powder
½ teaspoon baking soda
2 tablespoons Callebaut unsweetened cocoa (if other
   cocoa, double amount)
1 egg
1 teaspoon pure vanilla extract
½ cup sour cream
3-inch doughnut cutter
Paper towels or egg cartons for absorbing excess oil

For chocolate icing:

¾ cup confectioners' sugar
2 tablespoons Callebaut cocoa
½ teaspoon lemon juice
1 egg white
2 teaspoons water

Preheat the 3 inches of oil in your heavy pot to around 320
degrees. Use the thermometer.

Beat the brown sugar and butter together, using the
standing mixer and paddle attachment, until creamed. In a
large bowl, sift together the 2 cups flour, salt, baking powder,
baking soda, and cocoa. Beat the egg and vanilla together,
then add to the mixer, beating to combine.

In the adding, beating, stopping, scraping-down sequence,
add one-third of the flour to the mixer, then one-half sour
cream, then one-third flour, one-half sour cream, one-third
flour. Don't overbeat!

Bring the dough together onto your board—flour if the
dough is sticky—and roll out to ½ inch thickness. Using the

doughnut cutter, cut out the doughnuts from the edge, rolling inward with the cutter. Flour the cutter if the dough sticks to it. Save the holes for cooking too. If the area of your kitchen is warm, place the doughnuts on a lightly floured baking sheet, and put them in the refrigerator for 15 to 20 minutes. Cooler dough is easier to handle.

Check the temperature of the oil. Bring it up to 375 degrees. Try to ease it up there—if the oil gets too hot, it will start to smoke, and that's not good. You can also check to see if the oil's hot enough by dropping in a chunk of bread—it should immediately bob to the surface, lightly browned.

Put the doughnuts in the hot oil 2 or 3 at a time, depending on the size of your pot. They should be able to move around in the oil. Cook 3 to 4 minutes on the first side, turn and cook another 2 to 3 minutes on the second. Make sure your wire spoon is dry—no water should ever come in contact with the hot oil; severe burns from spattering could result. As the doughnuts are finished, transfer them to a paper towel.

Turning to the ingredients for the icing, sift the confectioners' sugar and cocoa together into a bowl. Add the remaining ingredients and whisk together until smooth. You can spread the icing on the doughnuts after they have cooled for about 10 minutes.

DANISH

Prune Danish

Makes 8

*D*anishes are one of the bigger challenges in baking. The mixing is like that for biscuits, the dough has to rise as a bread, and there's a lot of rolling out to do. You need to be precise with the details and delicate of touch. Scared yet?

I made these with a prune filling because it's so hard to find prune Danishes in the coffee shops and bakeries anymore, and I love them. If you would like a cheese filling, see my recipe on page 48 for Cheese Blintze Filling.

We'll start with the filling because it needs time to cook and cool.

To make the prune filling:

Makes 1⅔ cups

⅔ **cup water**
1 **tea bag**
2 **cups prunes**
½ **cup orange juice**
¼ **cup dark brown sugar, packed**

In a small pot bring the water to a slow boil and add the tea bag and the prunes. Cook for 2 minutes, then remove the tea bag, squeezing its liquid back into the pot. Lower the heat and add the orange juice and the brown sugar. Stir to dissolve the sugar, cover, and cook over very low heat for 45 minutes. Check occasionally—you want them to stew, not burn. Let the prunes cool, remove the pits, and puree them in the food processor.

To make the pastry dough:

1 packet dry yeast
4 tablespoons warm water (110 degrees)
Pinch sugar
3 cups all-purpose flour
1 teaspoon salt
1 tablespoon baking powder
2 tablespoons sugar
1 egg
1 teaspoon pure vanilla extract
½ cup scalded milk
4 tablespoons shortening (I used Crisco)
2 tablespoons melted butter, for the bowl and for brushing
2 sticks (1 cup) butter, cold
¼ cup slivered almonds
3 tablespoons apricot or peach jam
1 teaspoon lemon juice
2 teaspoons water

Gently stir the yeast into the warm water with the pinch of sugar—use a wooden or plastic spoon—and set in a warm spot to foam up for 3 to 5 minutes.

Combine the flour, salt, baking powder, and 2 tablespoons of sugar. Beat the egg with the vanilla and mix with the warm milk. Make sure the milk is just warm to the touch; if it's too hot it will cook the egg.

In a large bowl, add the shortening to the flour in dollops, combing it through with your fingers until you reach a crumbly texture. Add one-third of the flour to the bowl of a standing mixer fitted with the paddle. Add one-half of the liquid and beat just enough to combine. Stop and scrape down the sides with a spatula. Add one-third more flour and beat to combine. Stop and scrape. Add the rest of the liquid and beat to combine. Stop and scrape. Add the final third of the flour and beat to combine. Stop and check for any pockets of dry mix. Turn the mixer on again. The dough should come together around the paddle stem.

Place the dough in a large glass bowl with about 1 table-spoon of the melted butter. Roll to coat the dough and cover with a clean towel. Set aside in a warm spot to rise for about 20 minutes.

Cut each butter stick into 2 equal parts. Cut each part into small cubes about ¼ inch on each side. Keep the 4 portions of butter separate.

Have some flour on hand for dusting the board and rolling pin. It can be helpful to spread plastic wrap over the board and put the dough on top of it. Knead the dough a little to get a silky texture. Roll out into a rectangle 12 x 7 inches, working good right angles at the four corners. Visually draw two lines from one long side to the other, dividing the dough into thirds. Cover the middle and one other third with one portion of the butter cubes. Fold the unbuttered third over the buttered middle and then fold the remaining buttered third over that one. Now turn the dough (or the plastic wrap) 90 degrees counterclockwise (from six o'clock to three o'clock) and again roll out to 12 x 7 inches. Repeat with the second portion of butter: fold in, turn, roll out, continuing through the third and fourth portions, until all the butter has been used.

If at any point the butter starts coming out the sides, you can chill the dough for 20 minutes or so in the refrigerator before continuing.

Roll the dough out into a neat-cornered rectangle 12 x 3 inches. Out of this you can cut 7 triangles with 3-inch sides, plus 2 end pieces that you can pinch together for the 8th tri-angle. You might want to create a paper template of a 3-inch equilateral triangle to make this easier.

Brush each triangle with some melted butter and spoon on 1½ to 2 tablespoons of the prune filling. Spread it with the back of the spoon. Bring the points of the triangles together and pinch them closed and pinch the seams together. Now press almond slivers into the seams and tops of the pastries. Place them on a greased baking sheet or a baking sheet using a nonstick sheet. Let them rise for 20 minutes.

Preheat the oven to 350 degrees.

Melt the jam, lemon juice, and water together over a low heat and brush onto the Danishes. Bake in the oven for 25 to 30 minutes, until they are golden brown.

Well, how did you do? Now you know why it's hard to find prune Danishes in this age of the "quick and easy."

Ginger Ale–Pear Turnovers

Makes 4

Seppi Renggli, the chef I apprenticed under at the Four Seasons, taught me to impart a subtle ginger flavor to certain fruits and vegetables by poaching them in ginger ale. It is a wonderful way to prepare apples and pears for turnovers and Danishes. It's equally terrific with carrots, but that's for another cookbook.

As you will learn in a later chapter (see Ratatouille Turnovers, p. 185), puff pastry is handy to have in the freezer. We don't attempt to make it ourselves. The French use it to make mille-feuilles, or thousand sheets, a hyperbolic expression of its multiple layers of butter and pastry. However, if we did try to make it, it would seem a thousand times harder than the Danish dough in the previous recipe.

To make the filling:

4 medium pears, peeled, cored, and cubed (about 3 cups)
2 teaspoons lemon juice
3 tablespoons dark brown sugar
⅓ cup ginger ale
1 teaspoon cinnamon

Put everything in a medium pot, bring to a boil, stir, then reduce heat and cook for 15 minutes until the pears are tender. Let cool before using in turnovers.

To make the turnovers:

½ **teaspoon cinnamon**
1 **tablespoon sugar**
1 **egg**
2 **tablespoons butter**
Defrost enough puff pastry to make 4 six-inch square
   pieces

Preheat the oven to 400 degrees.

Prepare a baking sheet with vegetable spray or use a non-stick sheet.

Mix the cinnamon and sugar together. Beat the egg separately. Cut the butter into 4 portions of very small pieces.

Save any strips of pastry left over from cutting out the 4 six-inch squares. Roll out the squares to 7 inches. Brush a wash of the egg over the squares, avoiding the very edge. Having divided the pear filling into 4 portions, put 1 portion onto a triangular half of each of the squares. Dot a portion of butter over the filling of each turnover. Fold the uncovered triangles over the filling and, using the tines of a fork, stitch the seams of the turnovers closed.

Brush the turnovers with more of the egg, sprinkle them with cinnamon-sugar, and poke a steam slit into each with the point of a knife. Place them on a baking sheet and bake for 10 minutes at 400 degrees. Lower the heat to 325 and bake for another 10 minutes.

If you have scraps of pastry dough, brush with egg, sprinkle with cinnamon-sugar, twist them, and bake for about 10 minutes until light brown. They will make a tasty little snack to have with tea in the afternoon.

Popovers

Makes 10

*T*hese *little balloons have to sit in a turned-off oven after they are done. With all the roasting and baking we do at the restaurant, we never turn our ovens off, so we don't make them there. There is an establishment three blocks north of Good Enough that takes its name from this product.*

If you've ever had an éclair, choux, or profiterole, this is the dough they are made with. Popover tins are available, but you can just as easily use a muffin pan.

1 cup all-purpose flour
½ teaspoon salt
2 eggs
1 tablespoon melted butter plus additional for greasing
  pan
1 cup milk

Preheat the oven to 425 degrees and place the buttered muffin pan inside to heat.

Sift the flour together with the salt. Beat the eggs well with a fork. Put all ingredients in a large bowl and beat together until it's as smooth as mayonnaise. (I used a hand-held electric mixer for this.)

Take the pan out of the oven and fill each cup halfway with batter. Bake in the oven for 30 minutes. Turn off the oven and prick the tops of the popovers with a fork. Let them sit in the oven for another 10 minutes. Serve immediately. They can be filled with whipped cream, or with some vanilla ice cream, and topped with a drizzle of chocolate syrup.

✦✦✦✦✦✦✦✦✦ NINE ✦✦✦✦✦✦✦✦✦

Jams, Preserves, and Marmalades

Glossary:

- ♥ Jelly is made with fruit juice, pectin, and sugar.
- ♥ Jam is jelly with fruit pulp.
- ♥ Preserves are jam with chunks of fruit.
- ♥ Marmalade is a citrus jelly with peel.
- ♥ Compote is fruit cooked in fruit syrup.

Preserves are so named because the heat of cooking kills the microbes present in the fruit, and the sugar acts as a preservative.

As jams derive their flavor from the fruit you use, be careful to select fruit that is perfectly ripe, flavorful, and of high quality. It is the reaction of the acids in fruit with pectin that "sets" jams. Various fruits have more or less pectin: Strawberries are low, apples and cranberries are high. The pits and pith of fruits generally have the most pectin, and that is why you have the jelly bag—to cook the pectin out of them and into the jam or marmalade. Sugar also acts as a setting agent. If you wish to use less sugar, you can buy pectin in health food stores. Follow the instructions on the package.

You will need a large, heavy pot (8 quarts), candy thermometer, long-handled wooden spoon, jelly bag (or a piece of cheesecloth to make one), 4 pint-sized mason jars, and parchment paper for sealing the jars.

I would also suggest you wear long sleeves and use an oven mitt to protect your hand and arm from a possible spatter of hot sugar.

The following are recipes for jams and marmalades that I think are particularly good with breakfast. Other berries could be substituted in the Strawberry Jam recipe, citrus fruits other than oranges could be used in the Orange-Bourbon Marmalade recipe, and other pitted fruits could be used in the Peach-Ginger Preserves.

Strawberry Jam

Makes about 7 cups

4 mason jars
1 lemon zested; the rest peeled, seeded, and sliced
1 large apple, peeled, cut up (save peel, core, and seeds
   for jelly bag)
3 pounds strawberries (leaves and stems removed)
¾ pounds (1½ cups) granulated sugar
6 tablespoons fresh or dry cranberries
Parchment paper

Preheat the oven to 250 degrees.

Sterilize the mason jars and lids by running them through a dishwasher, or boil them for 20 minutes, then cover them with a clean towel. Place the jars in the preheated oven at 250 degrees. Heat the jars for 20 minutes. (Besides being sterilized, the jars need to be hot to receive the hot jam.)

After grating the zest off the lemon, cut off the pith (white outside) and slice the lemon thinly, removing the seeds. Put the seeds and pith in the jelly bag with the peel, core, and seeds of the apple. (If you don't have a jelly bag, fashion one from a piece of cheesecloth and tie off with a string.)

In the 8-quart pot, mash one-third of the strawberries with one-half of the sugar and the apple, cranberries, and lemon slices and zest. Simmer until the sugar is dissolved with the juice from the fruit, stirring regularly. This should take about 6 to 7 minutes, after which add the jelly bag.

Put the rest of the sugar into a 9-inch cake pan and heat it in the oven for about 7 minutes. (Check the sugar to make sure it stays loose—you don't want it to get hard.)

Just before you add the heated sugar and the rest of the fruit to the pot, remove the jelly bag and squeeze it out completely into the pot.

When all ingredients are in the pot, stir and bring to a rolling boil. Stir and cook for about 17 minutes, continuing to boil. Put in a candy thermometer. The jam should set when the mixture hits 220 degrees. The white foam on top is normal, but if you notice any scum on top of the foam, skim it off and discard. Take the jam off the heat to cool for 15 minutes.

Ladle the jam into the hot jars and let cool for 10 minutes. Place a round of parchment paper over the top of each of the jars and screw on the lids tightly.

The jam will store for 6 months to a year in a cool, dry place away from sunlight. Once opened, it needs to be refrigerated.

Cranberry Preserves

Makes 3 cups

Since this recipe makes half the amount of the Strawberry Jam, you needn't go to the trouble of sterilizing mason jars for long storage. Cranberry Preserves will keep very well in a covered container for 3 weeks in the refrigerator.

¾ cup dark brown sugar (packed for measurement)
2 tablespoons honey
4 cups fresh or frozen cranberries (pick through for any
    green or blemished berries)
Wedge of lime (⅛ of a whole lime) stuck with 3 cloves
1 teaspoon cinnamon
1 cup pineapple juice
Small pinch (combined) salt and pepper

Preheat the oven to 250 degrees. Heat the brown sugar in the oven in a baking pan for about 5 minutes. Check to make sure the sugar doesn't start to crust over during heating.

Reserve the honey (which should never be cooked), and put into a large, heavy pot (8 quarts, at least), over low heat, the cranberries, lime, cinnamon, pineapple juice, salt and pepper, and the heated brown sugar. You don't need additional pectin because the cranberries have plenty.

Simmer, stirring frequently, using a long-handled wooden spoon and oven mitt. (Please observe the precaution of using the long wooden spoon and oven mitt—sugar burns are the worst!)

Continue cooking until the sugar has dissolved and the fruit has released its juices.

Raise the heat and bring the mixture to a rolling boil, then reduce and simmer for 25 to 30 minutes, stirring frequently. Use a candy thermometer at this point to determine when your mixture gets to 220 degrees, which is the setting temperature. If you see any scum at the top, skim it off and discard.

Allow the jam to cool for ½ hour and stir in the honey.
Ladle into a container, cover, and refrigerate.

Peach-Ginger Preserves

Makes 6 to 7 cups

*There's barely a whit of difference between a jam and a pre-
serve, and some people use the words interchangeably. I call this
a preserve because I make it with large pieces of peach. If the
peaches were run through the processor, I guess I'd have to call
it a jam or perhaps a "butter." Words, words, words . . . !*

5 pounds peaches (half of them ripe, half not quite;
   yields 4 pounds peeled, pitted, and quartered)
1½ pounds sugar (about 3 cups)
4 mason jars for storage
8 fresh cardamom pods
1 lemon, zested, pith removed, sliced thinly, seeds
   removed (keep pith and seeds for bag)
1 apple, cored, peeled, and cut into chunks (peel and core
   for jelly bag)
3 tablespoons crystallized ginger (finely sliced)
Parchment paper

Cut the peeled peaches into quarters (larger or smaller, as you
like) and combine with half the sugar. (Reserve the peels and
pits for the jelly bag.) Stir to coat, cover with plastic wrap,
and refrigerate for 24 hours.

The next day, preheat the oven to 250 degrees. Sterilize
the mason jars and lids by running them through the dishwasher (or boiling them for 20 minutes), then heating in
oven for 20 minutes.

In an 8-quart pot over low heat, simmer the sugared
peaches for 10 minutes, until the sugar is dissolved, stirring

frequently with a long wooden spoon. Bring to a boil, then simmer for another 15 to 20 minutes.

Heat the remainder of the sugar in a cake pan in the oven for about 7 minutes, making sure it doesn't crust over.

Split the cardamom pods with the back of a knife and put them in the jelly bag along with the lemon pith and seeds, the apple peel and core, peach pits, and sliced ginger. Add the jelly bag and the heated sugar to the pot and stir in. Add the apple chunks and lemon slices and zest and stir.

Bring to a boil, then reduce heat and simmer for about 1 hour or until your candy thermometer reaches 220 degrees. Skim off any scum that may appear.

Remove from heat and take out the jelly bag and squeeze out by pressing it against the inside of the pot with the spoon. Stir several times and let the mixture cool for 15 minutes. Ladle the preserves into the heated mason jars and let cool, uncovered, for 10 minutes.

Cover the jars with parchment rounds, screw the lids on tightly, and turn upside down for 10 minutes. This will help the peaches distribute evenly.

Store in a sunless, dry, cool place. The preserves will keep for up to 1 year. Once opened, refrigerate.

Orange-Bourbon Marmalade

Makes about 5 cups

I want to express my thanks to Grand-père Colin, the father-in-law of my friend Christina, who relayed to me his invaluable advice on making marmalade. It takes time and space in the refrigerator, so be prepared.

4 pounds (about 8) slightly underripe oranges
½ pound (2) lemons
2½ pounds (5 cups) sugar

⅓ **cup bourbon**
3 pint-sized mason jars
Parchment paper

Slice the ends off all the oranges and lemons. Slice the peel, including the pith, off 2 oranges and cut into chunks, removing the pits and saving the juice. Discard the peel, pith, and seeds from the oranges. Now slice the rest of the unpeeled oranges and the lemons wafer thin. Retain the juice and seeds with the slices in a large bowl. Cover the fruit with water (about 5 cups), then cover the bowl with a plate and place in the refrigerator for 24 hours.

The next morning (if you started in the morning!) preheat the oven to 250 degrees. Sterilize the mason jars and lids by running them through the dishwasher or boiling them for 20 minutes. Then place them in the oven for another 20 minutes.

Put the fruit and water in a heavy 8-quart pot, bring to a boil, and cook at boiling for 30 minutes, stirring regularly. Place the sugar in a cake pan and heat it in the oven for 5 to 7 minutes.

Reduce the heat under the pot and stir in the heated sugar until it is dissolved. Increase the heat and bring to a rolling boil. Stir regularly, wearing an oven mitt. Cook this way for 25 to 30 minutes, until the candy thermometer reads 220 degrees, then turn off the heat and let cool for 10 minutes.

Heat the bourbon in a small saucepan to barely boiling and remove. Stir the bourbon into the cooling marmalade. Once this is done and the 10-minute cooling period is up, stir the mixture once and ladle into the heated mason jars. Try to disperse the fruit evenly between them.

Put on parchment paper rounds and seal the jars tightly. Turn them upside down for 10 minutes to disperse the fruit throughout the marmalade. As with other preserves, store in a cool, dry place, free from exposure to direct sunlight. Once you open a marmalade, you must refrigerate it.

Boy, is this stuff good on biscuits, toast, or scones!

Apricot Compote

Makes 1¾ cups

Compote *means stewed fruit in French, and that's what it means in English as well. This is a shortcut jam that has a variety of uses. Spoon it over pancakes or waffles, use it as a filling for blintzes, or use it as a kind of chutney with pork chops or baked ham.*

½ lemon
6 apricots (½ pound), pitted and quartered
Zest of 1 orange
½ cup orange juice
2 to 3 tablespoons dark brown sugar
Pinch salt
Pinch black pepper
1 tablespoon Grand Marnier (optional)

Squeeze the ½ lemon and drop it, along with the juice, into a fairly large, heavy saucepan. Add all the rest of the ingredients except the Grand Marnier, and bring to a boil.

Reduce the heat and simmer, stirring occasionally with a wooden spoon, for 45 minutes.

Strain the mixture, removing the lemon and reserving the apricots in a bowl. Put the liquid back into the pot and boil for about 10 minutes, stirring frequently, until it becomes a thick syrup. If desired, stir in the Grand Marnier at this point.

Combine the apricots with the syrup and use as a topping, filling, or sweet condiment.

Apple Butter

Makes 4 to 6 cups

The yield of this recipe will be closer to 6 cups in the fall when the apples are right off the trees and have their maximum water content. The spring and early summer apples have been in storage and will yield less.

Apple Butter is used as a spread for toast, biscuits, English muffins, and should be thought of as a jam: It contains no butter and has the high sugar content of a fruit preserve or a jam.

3 pint-sized mason jars
1 cup water
1 cup apple cider
Pinch salt
4 pounds Granny Smith or McIntosh apples, skins on,
    cored and quartered
3 pounds (6 cups) dark brown sugar
1½ teaspoons cinnamon
¼ teaspoon ground cloves
¼ teaspoon allspice
Zest and juice of 1 lemon
Parchment paper

Preheat the oven to 250 degrees. Run the mason jars through the dishwasher or boil them for 20 minutes to sterilize. Place them in the oven for another 20 minutes. If you're not going to put the Apple Butter in storage, it will keep well in a tightly covered container in the refrigerator for up to 2 weeks.

In a large, heavy pot, combine the water, cider, and salt and bring to a boil. Add the apple quarters, stir, and simmer for about 15 minutes, until the apples are soft. Remove the apples with a slotted spoon, place in a large bowl, and remove and discard their skins. Reserve the liquid in a separate container.

Blend the apples in a food processor until smooth. Now determine how many cups of apple you have, and measure out ½ cup of brown sugar for each cup of apple. Put the sugar in the pot together with ¼ cup of the reserved liquid, the cinnamon, cloves, and allspice. Stir well and dissolve the sugar over a very low heat (about 10 minutes).

Once the sugar is dissolved, add the remainder of the reserved liquid, the lemon zest and juice, and the processed apple. Stir well and bring to a boil. Reduce to a very low heat and cook, covered, for about 3 hours, stirring occasionally. The Apple Butter will darken.

Let the butter cool for 15 minutes before transferring to containers. If storing, ladle into the heated mason jars, let cool for another 10 minutes, then seal tightly with parchment rounds and lids. Store in a cool, dry location, away from direct sunlight. Once opened, store in refrigerator.

TEN

Breakfast Meats

In this chapter I give you recipes for the preparation of bacon, sausage, hashes, and ham—the traditional breakfast meats on our menu at Good Enough to Eat.

Bacon

My butcher supplies me with a double-smoked, nonsulfite bacon, and I cut 6 to 8 slices per pound. I recommend that you initiate a friendly relationship with your neighborhood butcher. He can be tremendously helpful to you with these recipes.

Besides buying great, preservative-free bacon, using a sprinkle of sugar provides the "magic" of this bacon. I get more raves from customers for my bacon than for any other single item on the menu. At least it seems that way. Clara, a schoolmate of my second son, Asa, asked him to bring her some of my bacon to her birthday party as a present. So Asa brought 2 pounds of it to the party with the recipe for preparing it. Asa was embarrassed, but Clara was thrilled.

8 rashers of bacon
2 teaspoons of cane (sugar-in-the-raw) or light brown
   sugar

Prepared in the oven:
   This is the way we cook the bacon at the restaurant.
   Preheat the oven to 450 degrees. Place the rashers (slices)
of bacon on a cutting board and scrape them out with the
back of a knife. This retards shrinkage. Place the rashers on a
baking sheet and sprinkle each with a very slight amount of
sugar. Bake in the oven for about 20 minutes, more or less,
depending on how well done and crunchy you like your
bacon.
   Remove the bacon from the pan onto some paper towels
to blot up the excess fat. Serve with practically anything else
on the breakfast menu.

Prepared on the griddle or in the pan:
   Preheat the griddle to high heat. (A frying pan should be
preheated as well, although it will heat faster than the
griddle.)
   Scrape out the bacon as described above, and place on the
griddle. Sprinkle each slice with a little bit of sugar. Turn
the rashers after 5 minutes and sprinkle a very little sugar on the
second side. Turn again after another 5 minutes and flatten
the bacon with a spatula. Continue to turn and flatten for
another 10 minutes, until the bacon is cooked the way you
like it.
   Remove the bacon to some paper towels and blot away the
excess fat. Serve.

Pork Sausage

Makes 8 patties

Ask your butcher for ground pork for sausage patties. This should be a mixture of pork butt or shoulder and 20 percent fat. Make sure the butcher understands that the pork is for sausage and not meat loaf.

The less you handle ground meat, the better. This is true for hamburger meat and meat loaf as well. See my recipe for meat loaf in my first book, Good Enough to Eat: Bountiful Home Cooking (see bibliography). Never squeeze ground meat or press down on it when it's cooking. If you happen to notice a deep pink or purplish color about the time the sausage is done, don't worry about it.

¼ cup boiling water
1½ teaspoons dark brown sugar
1¾ teaspoons kosher salt
1 teaspoon black pepper
¼ teaspoon dried sage
2 pounds ground pork for sausage
1 tablespoon chopped parsley

If cooking in the oven, preheat it to 400 degrees. Or preheat the griddle to medium-high. Once the water has boiled, put it in a bowl and add the brown sugar, salt, pepper, and sage. Stir to dissolve the salt and sugar.

Put the sausage meat in a large bowl and poke some holes in it with a finger. Drizzle the water mixture over the holes and sprinkle on the parsley. Now combine by combing your fingers through, or mix with a couple of salad forks. Don't squeeze! Keep the mixture loose. Make eight patties.

Place the patties on the baking sheet and cook in the oven for 15 to 20 minutes without turning. If using a griddle or frying pan, make sure it is hot before putting on the patties. Turn once, when the juices start to bubble up at the top of the pattie. Make sure they cook through, but don't overcook, and don't press down on them with the spatula.

Place on paper towels when done to absorb excess fat. Serve.

Turkey Sausage

Makes 8 five-inch patties

Some people eat only white meat, others only dark. For sausage, however, it's best to have both. Dark meat has a little more fat than the white, and the flavor is in the fat. Ask your butcher to grind both for turkey sausage. As with all ground meats: minimal handling and no squeezing! I also use a little vegetable oil for the pan or griddle because turkey meat is low in fat. If the oil is very hot, hardly any of it will get into the sausage pattie.

1½ teaspoons kosher salt
½ teaspoon black pepper
½ teaspoon dried sage
2 teaspoons chopped parsley
¼ cup warm water
½ cubed stale white or French bread (crust removed)
¼ cup scalding milk
2 pounds ground turkey
1 tablespoon vegetable oil

Preheat the oven to 400 degrees or the griddle to medium-high. If you're using a frying pan, make sure you heat it medium-high before putting in the patties.

Put the herbs and spices into the warm water in a bowl. (Heat the water in a microwave for 30 seconds.) Stir and let sit.

Add the bread cubes to the milk you have brought to scalding.

Put the ground turkey into a large mixing bowl and poke holes into the surface with your finger. Drizzle the water-spice mixture over the turkey and comb it in with your fingers or two salad forks. Then add the milk-bread mixture and combine in the same way.

Make patties 5 inches by ¾ inch. Oil the baking pan (or the griddle or frying pan) and place the patties on the pan. Cook in the oven for 15 minutes without turning or pushing down. On the griddle or pan, turn when the first side is well seared. You'll see juices start to appear on the top surface. Turn only once and don't press down on them. Cook for about 15 minutes.

Place on paper towels after removing from oven or griddle to soak up any excess fat. Serve.

Cooked Turkey Sausage (once cool) can be wrapped in plastic, then aluminum foil, and stored in the freezer for up to 2 months. Defrost in the refrigerator compartment. Brush with a little butter before reheating in a frying pan or on the griddle (the oven could dry them out).

Tarragon Chicken Livers

Makes 4 servings

These are great with Spoonbread (p. 180). You can also puree them in a food processor and have a spread for crackers or apple wedges. A wok is ideal for cooking chicken livers, but you can also use a heavy frying pan or cast-iron skillet. The important thing is to cook the livers at a consistent, high heat.

1 pound chicken livers
3 scallions
½ cup all-purpose flour
1 teaspoon kosher salt
½ teaspoon coarse ground black pepper
1 tablespoon butter
1 teaspoon vegetable oil (added to the butter)
2 teaspoons dried tarragon or 1 tablespoon fresh
   (or substitute dill)

Clean the livers and rinse in cold water. Pat dry with paper towel. Remove the root ends of the scallions and cut them into 1-inch pieces (green parts, too).

Combine the flour, salt, and pepper and dredge the livers, shaking off any excess.

Heat the butter and oil in a wok or skillet. When it is hot and bubbling, add the chicken livers and cook for 3 minutes, shaking the pan close to the heat to keep the livers moving. Add the tarragon, rubbing it between the thumb and fore-finger as you sprinkle it in. If fresh tarragon, you don't need to rub it. Add the scallions. Mix in, turning the livers, keeping them separated.

After cooking 3 to 4 minutes with the herbs, and when they're nice and brown, serve on wedges of toast or with Spoonbread.

Turkey Hash

Makes 4 servings

This recipe will come in handy after roast turkey holidays like Christmas and Thanksgiving. See Roast Turkey on page 173.

2 pounds new potatoes
1 teaspoon kosher salt plus a pinch for the potatoes
4 tablespoons butter
½ teaspoon cracked black pepper
½ rounded teaspoon paprika
⅛ teaspoon cayenne pepper
Pinch nutmeg
1 cup onion, cut into ½-inch cubes
½ cup celery, cut into ½-inch cubes
½ cup carrot, cut into ½-inch cubes
½ cup red pepper, seeded, white removed, cut into
    ½-inch cubes
¾ pound (1 cup) turkey, cut cross-grain into 1½-inch
    pieces
¼ cup white wine (or water)

Cover the potatoes with water in a large pot with a pinch of salt and bring to a boil, covered. Once boiling, uncover, reduce heat, and cook in rolling water about 20 minutes, until tender. Rinse the potatoes in cold water and cut them into 1-inch cubes.

In a large cast-iron skillet, melt the butter together with the 1 teaspoon salt, pepper, paprika, cayenne, and nutmeg over high heat. After about 2 minutes, when the paprika has darkened and a nutty aroma develops, add the vegetables. Stir with a wooden spoon, scraping the bottom of the pan, and cook for 2 to 3 minutes.

Add the potatoes and stir to coat them. Add the turkey and stir until hot. Drizzle the wine into areas of the pan where things are sticking, and scrape with the wooden spoon. Continue deglazing until all the wine has evaporated and the Turkey Hash is done.

Serve it on whole-wheat toast with a poached egg on top.

Corned Beef Hash

Makes 4 servings

We serve Corned Beef Hash year-round at Good Enough to Eat. You might find the recipe particularly useful the day after Saint Patrick's Day. See my recipe for preparing Corned Beef on page 172.

2 pounds new potatoes, quartered after they are boiled
1 teaspoon kosher salt plus a pinch for the potatoes
4 tablespoons butter
½ teaspoon black pepper
1½ teaspoons paprika
¼ teaspoon red pepper flakes
1 cup onion cut into ½-inch cubes
1 cup green pepper, seeded, white removed, cut into
     ½-inch cubes
¾ pound (1 cup) corned beef, cut into 1-inch cubes

Preheat the oven to 500 degrees.

Cover the potatoes with water in a large pot with a pinch of salt, cover, and bring to a boil. Once boiling, uncover, reduce heat, and continue to cook in rolling water for about 20 minutes, until tender but firm. Rinse in cold water and slice into quarters or a little smaller, if your potatoes are large.

In a large cast-iron skillet, melt the butter together with 1 teaspoon salt, pepper, paprika, and red pepper flakes over a high heat. When the butter starts to brown—the milk solids in the butter, the paprika, and the pepper flakes will darken—add the onion and green pepper. Stir with a wooden spoon to coat the vegetables, and cook for 2 to 3 minutes, until the onion becomes brown.

Add the potatoes and stir into the mixture. Put in the corned beef cubes and stir. Cook for another minute, until the potatoes and corned beef are hot. Drizzle a little water into areas where things are sticking and scrape to deglaze. Now stick the whole skillet in the oven for 10 minutes to blend the flavors and get the hash a little crunchy. Be careful of the hot handle when taking it out.

Serve with two biscuits and a poached egg. I like this with a little ketchup.

Red Flannel Hash

Makes 4 servings

This is a vegetarian hash and as such doesn't belong in a chapter on breakfast meats, but it is prepared in the same way as the Turkey Hash, so I'm including it here. I replace the turkey with beets.

To cook the beets:

1 bay leaf
1 tablespoon dark brown sugar
1 fresh ancho chile or pinch of red pepper flakes
1 teaspoon salt
1 tablespoon red wine vinegar
1 teaspoon black pepper
1¼ pounds beets with 1 inch of stems on

Bring enough water to cover the beets to a boil in a large heavy pot with all the ingredients except the beets. Let boil for 10 minutes, then add the beets and bring back to a boil. Do not cut off that inch of stem! Cutting into the flesh of the beet before boiling causes the beets to "bleed" and lose flavor.

Once the water has returned to a boil, reduce the heat and simmer for about 45 minutes. The beets should be tender but still firm enough for cutting into cubes.

Drain the liquid from the beets. Do not run cold water over them as you would do with potatoes. Let them cool in a bowl large enough to be handled. Now cut off the stems and peel them with a paring knife. Cut the beets into cubes approximately ½ inch on a side.

To make the Red Flannel Hash:
To the ingredients in the Turkey Hash recipe (p. 168)—omitting the turkey—add:

⅛ teaspoon cloves
¼ teaspoon cinnamon
½ teaspoon sugar

These should be cooked in the butter together with the salt, pepper, paprika, cayenne, and nutmeg. Follow the cooking instructions for Turkey Hash, substituting the beets for the turkey. Don't add the beets with the uncooked vegetables—they only need to be reheated!

Serve on toast with a poached egg.

Corned Beef

Makes 8 to 10 servings

The corned beef, or corned brisket, as it is sometimes called, that is obtainable at your butcher's or market is already "corned"—that's the way it comes. What we are going to do is cook an already-corned beef. It will come wrapped in heavy plastic with spices and juices and usually weighs anywhere from 8 to 15 pounds. Any one in that weight range will work for this process. You'll probably want to have a corned beef and cabbage dinner one night and save the leftover corned beef for Corned Beef Hash sometime during the next week.

If you just want the corned beef to make the hash, you can get it already cooked at your local delicatessen, or "deli," as we Noo Yawkahs call it.

1 corned beef, 8 to 10 pounds
5 whole cloves
½ onion, with its skin
3 to 4 garlic cloves
6 peppercorns
2 bay leaves
1 large carrot, peeled and cut in thirds

Take the corned beef out of its wrap and discard the liquid. You need not wash off the meat. Place it in a large, heavy pot and add enough water to cover it. Now take the beef out of the water and set it to the side.

Stick the 5 cloves into the onion. Mash the garlic cloves with the side of a knife. Add these together with the peppercorns, bay leaves, and pieces of carrot to the water. Bring to a boil. Now put in the corned beef. Don't cut any of the fat off just yet, and be careful, don't splash! Bring back to a boil.

Reduce the heat and simmer, uncovered, for about 3 hours, until tender. Remove to the carving board. If there's any fat you want to get rid of, cut it off now. Slices should be cut across the grain of the meat and be about ⅓ inch thick. It's really good with some strong Dijon mustard.

Roast Turkey

Makes 8 to 10 servings

Thanksgiving is the most emblematic of special occasions at Good Enough to Eat. We roast about twenty large turkeys for the three reserved seatings in our fifty-seat restaurant. Perhaps because Thanksgiving symbolizes our spirit and decor so well, we have turkey dinner on the menu year-round. We are never short of freshly roasted turkey for our Turkey Hash.

1 fresh turkey (about 15 pounds)
4 tablespoons (½ stick) soft butter
1 tablespoon kosher salt
2 teaspoons black pepper
1 tablespoon dried sage
1 cup cooking sherry or white wine (optional)

Preheat the oven to 425 degrees.

Remove the extra fat from the turkey and discard. If the giblets are encased in plastic, take them out!

In a small bowl combine the butter, salt, pepper, and sage. Be sure to rub the sage between your fingers to release its flavor. With breast side up, rub the surface of the turkey with the butter mixture.

Place the turkey, breast side up, and the giblets in a roasting pan and place in the preheated oven.

Roast for 20 minutes before reducing the heat to 350 degrees. Baste the turkey with some wine, if you are using it, but be sure to use the drippings in the bottom of the pan for basting as well. Baste with wine and drippings every 20 minutes. A 15-pound turkey will take between 2½ and 3 hours to cook. You can check to see if it's done by pricking the skin under the drumstick—if the juice runs clear, it's done. If you have a meat thermometer, stick it into the thigh and look for a reading of 175 to 180 degrees. If the skin starts to get too brown and the turkey is not yet done, cover with tinfoil to prevent the skin from getting too crisp.

Let the turkey cool on the counter for 15 minutes before carving, and save those juices and giblets in the pan!

Turkey Gravy

Makes about 4 cups

The secret to perfect gravy is in cooking the flour and leaving no lumps. If you don't want to use the wine, add a little water or more stock.

**Neck, giblets, liver, and the drippings from the roasting
    pan from preparing Roast Turkey (preceding recipe)**
½ cup all-purpose flour (for each cup of drippings)
½ cup cooking sherry or red wine
4 cups chicken or turkey stock
Kosher salt to taste
Black pepper to taste
1½ tablespoons chopped parsley (optional)

After roasting the turkey, take the skin off the neck, discard, and strip off the meat. Cut this and the giblets and liver into small pieces (⅛ inch).

Measure the amount of drippings left in the roasting pan. If more than 1 cup, reduce to 1 cup. If less, use proportionally less flour (1 part flour to 2 parts drippings).

With the roaster pan on the range top over high heat, add the cup of drippings and the giblets to the pan. (A large, cast-iron skillet with a pouring spout would be ideal for this, if you have one.) Once things are very hot, add the flour and stir and scrape with a wooden spoon, to cook and eliminate any lumps in the flour. You are making a "roux"—the basis of any gravy.

The roux should brown, and you will detect a nutty aroma when it is ready. Whisk in the wine until it has reduced, then add the stock. Cook and continue whisking and reducing until the gravy thickens to the desired consistency. Taste it to see if you would like to add any more salt or pepper. Stir in the chopped parsley at the end.

Glazed Baked Ham

Makes 18 servings

It takes a long time to bake a ham. You'll need to start by noon to have the ham ready for dinner. The time will be well spent, however, as the ham will keep well in the refrigerator and will be so useful for many breakfasts and lunches.

If you don't have the time, you can buy a ham that has already been cooked. Put on the glaze and heat in a hot oven until the internal temperature of the ham reaches 140 degrees. You'll need a meat thermometer.

At the restaurant we use a cold-smoked Esquay ham that comes packed in water.

1 Esquay ham (about 17 pounds)
⅓ cup Dijon mustard
⅓ cup packed dark brown sugar
⅓ cup apricot jam (or Cranberry Preserves, p. 156, or
    Orange-Bourbon Marmalade, p. 158)
12 whole cloves

Preheat the oven to 300 degrees.

Unpack the ham and place it in a foil-lined roasting pan and cover the ham with foil. Bake for 4½ hours for a 17-pound ham.

Mix the mustard, brown sugar, and jam together to create the glaze.

Take out the ham and slice most of the fat (but not all!) from the outside. Score a diamond pattern grid on the ham with the point of a knife. Stick the cloves into the places where the lines cross, distributing them over the ham. Generously slather the glaze over the ham.

Turn the heat up to 425 degrees and bake the ham for another hour, uncovered. Check the ham with a meat thermometer—it should reach 160 degrees at the center when it is done. Total cooking time will be approximately 5½ hours, or 20 minutes per pound.

Let the ham cool for 20 minutes before carving. If you started at noon, you could have dinner ready by 6:00.

ELEVEN

Sides and Salads

SIDES

Here are some of the items on the restaurant's breakfast menu that are usually prefaced by *with*, as in Scrambled Eggs *with* Hash Browns, or Granola *with* Yogurt. Admittedly, *sides* is a catch-pot category. Based on my shaky premise, bacon and sausage should be listed here, but I included them in a separate chapter. People do order "Waffles with Bacon," and "Pancakes with Sausage." There are also those who will have hash browns with bacon or sausage with toast.

The point is that the term *sides* certainly does not denote diminishment in the hierarchy of the breakfast table. I have customers who have hash browns with bacon (or vice versa) every day, and they will roar if their order is not up to standard. I have come to appreciate these "lions." Their roaring invariably points me toward something that needs attention. The cooks, of course, find them awfully bothersome. We can use 100 pounds of new potatoes for hash browns over a three-day weekend, and their preparation might sometimes be rushed. I put comment cards on each table to facilitate communication between me and my "lions," and I answer each one personally.

Hash Brown Potatoes

Serves 4

2 pounds new potatoes (quartered)
1 teaspoon kosher salt, plus a pinch for the potatoes
4 tablespoons butter
½ teaspoon butcher's cracked black pepper
½ teaspoon paprika
⅛ teaspoon cayenne
Pinch nutmeg
1 cup onion, chopped in ½-inch cubes
1 cup green pepper, seeded, white cut out, cut in ¾-inch
   cubes

Preheat oven to 500 degrees.

Put the potato quarters into a large, heavy pot with enough cold water to cover, add a pinch of salt, cover, and bring to a boil. Once boiling, remove cover and reduce to medium and cook for approximately 20 minutes or until tender—just tender, not mushy. Drain and rinse under cold water.

In a large, heavy skillet with a metal handle, melt the butter with all the spices over high heat until the butter foams up and browns—it becomes *noisette* and emits a nutty aroma. Add the onion and green pepper, spread them evenly, and let them stick before stirring loose. (The sticking is good for flavor.) Cook for 5 minutes before adding the potatoes. Stir and turn them, making sure they pick up the goodies from the bottom of the pan. Cook another 5 minutes.

Put the pan into the oven for 10 to 15 minutes to get the hash browns crunchy. This is how hash browns are made at Good Enough, and I recommend it, based on a poll among my "lions." Be careful to use an oven mitt when taking the pan out of the oven. There is a tendency to forget that the handle is red-hot.

Serve *with*—well, I leave it up to you.

Grits

Serves 4

Hominy grits are made from corn and are as popular in the South as hash browns are in the North as a side with eggs. I include Grits to encourage you to try them. For anyone who is avoiding wheat, they make a delicious alternative.

¾ **cup grits**
3½ **cups cold water**
¼ **teaspoon salt**
Pinch black pepper
Butter, salt, and pepper for serving

Stir the grits into the cold water with the salt and pepper. Bring to a boil, then cover and cook over a very low heat for 15 minutes, stirring occasionally, until the grits have thickened. Remove from heat.

Serve with a generous amount of butter and salt and pepper to taste.

CHEESE GRITS

Add 4 tablespoons of coarsely grated cheddar cheese after grits have been removed from the heat. Stir in, cover, and let sit for a couple of minutes before serving.

Spoonbread

Makes 6 to 8 servings

I learned this recipe from my friend and neighbor, Norman, who was born and bred in rural Virginia. So named because, coming out of the oven, it is eaten with a spoon—usually with sautéed chicken livers or ham (see "Breakfast Meats"). After a day in the refrigerator, it becomes almost identical to corn bread in taste and texture. Norman says that it never got to the refrigerator at his house.

4 tablespoons (½ stick) butter
3 eggs, separated
1 cup coarsely ground yellow cornmeal
¼ cup all-purpose flour
½ teaspoon kosher salt
2 cups buttermilk
2 teaspoons baking powder

Preheat the oven to 400 degrees. Place a large cast-iron skillet or large frying pan with a metal handle in the oven and add the butter to it to melt.

In a large bowl, loosely combine the egg yolks, cornmeal, flour, salt, and buttermilk.

Whisk the egg whites to a soft peak. Put 1 tablespoon of the beaten whites into the cornmeal mixture and swirl it. This opens space in the mixture for the egg white, which you now fold in. Sprinkle on the baking powder, stirring through carefully.

Pour the batter into the heated pan with the butter. Bake for 10 minutes at 400 degrees, then lower to 350 degrees and bake for an additional 30 minutes, until golden. Testing, a knife should come out slightly wet but not sticky. Serve hot.

Broccoli Slaw

Makes 4 to 6 servings

I also got this recipe from our friend Norman, who taught us how to make Spoonbread (preceding recipe). I served it with a lunch for our neighbors and they all asked for the recipe. Here it is.

1 bunch broccoli
½ medium onion, chopped fine
3 stalks celery with leaves, chopped fine
½ cup sweet pickles (gherkins), chopped fine, with 1
    tablespoon of their juice
½ cup mayonnaise
1 tablespoon mustard
2 teaspoons red wine vinegar
1½ teaspoons celery seeds
½ teaspoon kosher salt
½ teaspoon coarse grind black pepper

Cut off the broccoli florets and peel the stalks. Now chop all the broccoli into small pieces, quite fine. Combine with the onion, celery, and pickles in a large bowl.

Whisk together the mayonnaise, mustard, wine vinegar, celery seeds, salt, and pepper in a separate bowl. Then mix with the vegetables and let sit for about an hour before serving.

Vegetarian Chorizo

Makes 8 patties

These are sausage substitutes for vegetarians. Note that the mix needs to "age" for 2 days, and you need a mortar and pestle.

2 garlic cloves
1 teaspoon cumin seeds
1 teaspoon black peppercorns
¼ cup balsamic vinegar
3 tablespoons chili powder
12 ounces (1 package) Yves Veggie Ground Round (most health food stores)
1 tablespoon olive oil

Put the garlic, cumin, and peppercorns into the mortar and mash to a paste with the pestle. Transfer the paste to a separate bowl, drizzle in the vinegar, add the chili powder and veggie round, and mix well. Cover the bowl with plastic wrap and let sit in the refrigerator for 48 hours.

On the third day, fashion the mixture into patty shapes (about 8). Heat the olive oil to medium-high in a frying pan. The veggie round is already cooked, so you just need to sear it on both sides and heat it through—about 3 to 4 minutes.

Serve as you would sausages with scrambled eggs or Scrambled Tofu.

Ratatouille

Makes 16 cups

Ratatouille can be cooked as a vegetable dish for part of a dinner course and then saved as a side dish with breakfast or used as a turnover filling. It involves quite a bit of preparation and yields a large amount of the stewed vegetables, so you should probably think of it for multiple uses.

½ cup olive oil, for sautéeing
2 teaspoons salt
¼ teaspoon black pepper
1 large onion, sliced into ¼-inch-thick half-moons
1 tablespoon chopped garlic
½ cup red wine
2 small eggplants (1 pound each), cut into 1-inch cubes
1 medium zucchini (10 ounces), stripe peeled, cut into
    ¼-inch-thick half-moons
1 medium yellow squash (10 ounces), cut into ¼-inch-
    thick half-moons
1 green pepper (about 6 ounces), seeded, white removed,
    cut into 1½-inch triangles
1 red pepper (6 ounces), seeded, white removed, cut into
    1½-inch triangles
1 can (32 ounces) plum tomatoes
2 teaspoons dried basil
2 teaspoons thyme
½ teaspoon dried rosemary, or 1 teaspoon chopped fresh
    rosemary
1 bay leaf

In a large cast-iron skillet or heavy frying pan, heat 2 tablespoons of the olive oil with ½ teaspoon of the salt and a pinch of the pepper. When the oil is hot and shimmering, add the onion and cook for about 10 minutes, until it starts to brown and stick to the pan. Add the garlic. Stir with a wooden spoon. Each time the onion starts to stick, deglaze by pouring in a little wine and scraping with the wooden spoon. Continue until all the wine is evaporated and the onion and garlic are tender but not mushy.

Remove the onion and garlic from the pan with a slotted spoon and reserve; drain the oil from them back into the pan. Add 2 more tablespoons of oil, ½ teaspoon of the salt, and a pinch of the pepper to the pan. Note that you are always adding to the old oil, not changing it.

When the oil is hot, add the eggplant cubes. Sauté, turning occasionally, for about 7 minutes, until eggplant is brown and tender. Remove with slotted spoon and place with the onions, making sure you drain the oil back into the pan.

Once again, add the same quantities of oil, salt, and pepper. Cook and reserve the squashes. Remember that the oil must be hot before you add the vegetables. The squash should take about 4 minutes.

Continue with the remaining oil, salt, pepper, and the green and red peppers. They will take about 10 minutes to brown lightly. Then return all the cooked, reserved vegetables to the pan. In a separate bowl, mash the plum tomatoes together with the basil, thyme, and rosemary. Remember to rub the dried herbs between your fingers to intensify their flavor. Add the tomatoes and herbs to the pan, and finally, the bay leaf.

Raise the heat and bring to a slow boil, then lower and simmer for about 20 more minutes. The Ratatouille is ready. Remove the bay leaf before serving.

Ratatouille Turnovers

Makes 6 to 24

These make very nice noshes for brunch or a cocktail party buffet. Creamed Spinach (p. 26) could replace the Ratatouille in this recipe. In either case you have a satisfying alternative to meat. To make bite-sized turnovers, use 3-inch pastry squares and 1 tablespoon of Ratatouille. For larger turnovers, use 7-inch squares and ¼ cup Ratatouille.

Parchment paper for pan, or nonstick sheets
1½ cups Ratatouille (p. 183)
Puff pastry sheets (at least 2)—you buy them frozen
1 egg, beaten for glaze

Preheat the oven to 400 degrees. Place parchment paper or nonstick sheet on a large baking sheet.

Pulse the Ratatouille in the food processor for a few seconds to reduce the size of the vegetable chunks—this is particularly important if you're making the small turnovers. For the large turnovers, cut the puff pastry sheets into six 6-inch squares and roll out each to 7 inches. For the smaller turnovers, cut out 24 squares, 2½ inches on a side, and roll them out to 3 inches.

Now visualize the triangular shape of the turnover: The square becomes two right triangles. One triangle becomes the bottom of the turnover, and one becomes the top (but don't cut them apart). Brush a little egg wash on the portion that will become the bottom triangle of the turnover—the one you will spoon the Ratatouille onto. Avoid the very edges of the dough, as the egg will make it hard to press the turnovers shut. The egg wash will keep the liquid from soaking into the pastry dough.

Spoon on the Ratatouille—¼ cup each for the 6 larger turnovers, 1 tablespoon each for the small ones. Fold over the tops and press the two sides closed with the tines of a fork.

Brush the tops of the turnovers with the egg glaze and poke a hole in the top of each with the point of a knife to let the steam out.

Place the turnovers on the baking sheet and bake in the 400-degree oven for 10 minutes. Reduce to 325 degrees and bake another 10 minutes, until browned.

The little turnovers are great for finger food. The large turnovers will make a meal. If you're planning to freeze the turnovers for future use, don't put the egg wash on the tops—inside is all right. Heat directly from the freezer, first brushing with egg wash, then placing in a 375-degree oven 10 to 15 minutes for the little ones, 20 to 25 minutes for the large.

Braised Tomatoes

Makes 4

Many years ago I had a supplier who called himself "Tomato Bob." He was actually an actor in his other life and an old friend of my husband's. At a certain time each year Bob would show up with the most beautiful tomatoes I'd ever seen. I think he personally searched the tomato farms in New Jersey for his select list of customers.

If you like tomatoes, you're already aware that you have to know where and when to look, smell them, and know the degree of ripeness you want. A good tomato is a treasure.

At the restaurant we serve these with our Sautéed Cornmeal Trout (p. 211).

4 large beefsteak tomatoes
2 tablespoons olive oil
1 teaspoon kosher salt
½ teaspoon cracked black pepper
1 tablespoon chiffonade of basil
½ teaspoon thyme
1 tablespoon red or white wine

These tomatoes can be cooked under a broiler or in the oven or using a combination of both. They will take about 7 minutes under the broiler, 15 minutes in the oven, and out of the oven and under the broiler for 1 to 2 minutes to get the tops a little crunchy.

Preheat the oven to 375 degrees.

Slice about ½ inch off the tops of the tomatoes.

Mix all the remaining ingredients together in a large bowl and roll the tomatoes in the mixture.

Place the tomatoes cut side up on a baking sheet and cook in the oven for about 15 minutes. Cooking time will vary with the ripeness of the tomatoes. You want them to get nice and hot throughout. The skins will wrinkle when they're ready. If you cook them only under the broiler, the tomatoes will naturally burn a little on the top—you'll have to keep an eye on them.

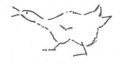

Prunes in Port

Makes 4 servings

Our anal-retentive society seems to be loosening up to the savor and health benefits of prunes. They are delicious, are good for constipation, and have more vitamin C than oranges. It's still probably wise not to eat too many at one sitting, however, so my portions per serving are small. Thirteen is my lucky number. (I know: Someone gets extra!)

13 pitted prunes
¼ cup port wine
1 cup water
1 tea bag

Combine the port, water, and tea bag and bring to a boil. Add the prunes. When the water comes back to a boil, remove the tea bag and squeeze it into the pot before discarding. Reduce heat and simmer for about 15 minutes, until done. The liquid should reduce to about ¼ cup.

Note: If you don't want to use the port, put a large slice of orange in with the prunes and add a little more water.

Serve with a little heavy cream or yogurt.

Low-Fat Homemade Yogurt

Makes 2 cups

This yogurt is easy to make if you have time and the space over a pilot light. To be truthful, we have neither at the restaurant, so we serve Brown Cow, an excellent whole-milk yogurt with live acidophilus cultures.

1½ cups warm water (110 to 115 degrees)
½ cup low-fat milk powder
1 heaping teaspoon yogurt with live acidophilus cultures

Put the water in the top part of a double boiler. Bring water in the bottom of the double boiler to a boil, then turn off the heat. Note: There should never be so much water in the bottom pan as to touch the bottom of the top pan.

Place the top pan with its water on top of the double boiler. When the temperature reaches 110 degrees, stir in the milk powder and the yogurt. Let the double boiler sit over a pilot light for between 8 and 12 hours. You may have to check the temperature—if the milk gets too hot, it will kill the cultures. Refrigerate before serving.

Serve with honey and wheat germ, over fruit or with granola.

Mock Crème Fraîche

Makes 2 cups

I'm not exactly sure how crème fraîche is made in France—I couldn't find a Frenchman who would tell me. This is close to what I remember it to be. It's good on fruit, waffles, smoked salmon, tarts, Swedish pancakes, and more. It's somewhere between sour cream and whipped cream in flavor and will keep for up to 3 weeks in the refrigerator.

1 cup sour cream
1 cup heavy cream

Whisk together to blend. Let sit in a covered container at room temperature for 24 hours or in the refrigerator for 48 hours . . . *et voilà!*

Bill makes a sweeter version of this by blending half plain yogurt with half vanilla ice cream. He has it on strawberries or blueberries, or with bananas, wheat germ, and honey.

FRUIT SALADS

Here I offer the Winter and Summer Fruit Salads that I serve at the restaurant. The composition of these depends upon the availability of fresh seasonal fruit and possibly upon the region of the country you live in. So my recipes are in that sense suggestions.

Fruit can be sweetened with honey or sugar; spiked with wine, liqueurs, or vodka; and served with yogurt, crème fraîche, or on its own. However you want to dress it up, the essential concern remains the quality of the fruit, and after that, how the fruit is cut and presented. I have a few tricks to share with you on these last three.

Every year in May we have the Amsterdam Street Fair and we have to prepare large quantities of fruit salad the day before. John Williams, a cook and poet who used to work for me, taught me how to store the fruit overnight. He put like kinds of prepared fruit in layers in wide plastic storage containers, with the softer fruit on top, and stored them in the walk-in. Only the bananas needed to be sliced and added for service on the next day.

Incidentally, if you put an apple with a bunch of bananas, the bananas will ripen much faster. You may want this or not! And if your brown sugar has turned into a brick, put a slice of apple or pear in with it overnight to restore the moisture and loosen it up.

Winter Fruit Salad

Serves 6

The proportions of the fruits can be juggled if you like. Bananas make a nice balance for acidy fruits such as citrus and strawberries, and since they are always available, I would recommend including them.

2 Granny Smith or McIntosh apples, or 2 Bosc pears
½ lemon, for juice
½ pound seedless green or red grapes
1 grapefruit
2 oranges
1½ cups strawberries (1 pint)
1 to 1½ cups pineapple chunks
2 ripe bananas

Slice the apples or pears into quarters, leaving the skins, and scoop out the cores. Cut into 1-inch chunks, squeeze the lemon's juice over them, and set aside. The lemon juice will keep the apples or pears from turning brown.

Wash the grapes or Blanche Du Bois will never eat your fruit salad. Pick out any grapes with blemishes.

To cut "supremes" from the grapefruit and oranges, work on a surface that will allow you to catch the juice. Cut off both ends of the fruit and stand it on one end. With a sharp paring knife, slice the peel and the white off, cutting down from top end to bottom. Once peeled, use the pointed end of the knife to cut the fruit sections out from between the membranes. Your knife has to be sharp or you will crush the juice out of the supremes.

Rinse the strawberries in cold water and pull off any leaves and stems with your fingers. If the strawberries are very dirty, let them sit in some water with a pinch of salt for a little while before giving a final rinse. Slice the strawberries in half, stem to stern.

Choose a pineapple at the market by tugging at the center leaves. The leaves will come out of a ripe one. Cut off the top and bottom, then cut in half crosswise. Wrap one piece in plastic wrap and save in the crisper. Using a sharp knife, slice off the outside of the pineapple the way you sliced off the outside of the oranges. Use the point of the knife to cut out the prickly spots. Now slice lengthwise in half and cut out the core. Cut into bite-sized chunks.

Cut the bananas into medallions and add at the very end of preparation. Toss together gently to avoid bruising, and serve. A drizzle of Cointreau, Grand Marinier, or kirsch wouldn't be amiss, if you're feeling up for something chic. Our customers have this as a main breakfast dish with a side of yogurt or cottage cheese.

Summer Fruit Salad

Serves 6

There is no citrus in our Summer Fruit Salad. Instead we use a lot of melons, berries, and bananas to replenish the minerals you lose by sweating. My husband used to run marathons, and he said that his favorite thing after a race was watermelon.

This salad is very beautiful, with a lot of variety in sizes, shapes, and textures and all those colors—reds, blues, greens, oranges, and yellows.

6 wedges of watermelon, about 4 inches wide at the rind
½ honeydew melon
½ cantaloupe
2 peaches
1 pint blueberries
1 pint strawberries
½ pineapple
3 ripe bananas

It's probably best to buy a piece of watermelon at the market. You can see if it's in good shape. But it's great to take a whole watermelon to the beach, where you don't have to worry so much about the mess.

Cut the honeydew and cantaloupe in half and scoop out the pits with a sharp-edged spoon. Turn the melons over on the flat side and slice the rind off in smooth strokes from top to bottom. Then slice the fruit about 1 inch thick.

Slice wedges of peach by cutting down to the pit from top to bottom in ½-inch intervals, then pull the wedges off the pit.

Rinse the blueberries, weed out any green or bad ones, and pick out any stray stems.

Rinse the strawberries, pull off the caps, and slice them in half.

When buying a pineapple, pull a couple center leaves to see if they're loose, and sniff the pineapple—it should smell ripe. Cut off the top and bottom and cut in half crosswise. Wrap up one half and put it in the crisper. Put the other half down on the larger flat end and, using a sharp knife, slice off the outer part, moving from top to bottom. Cut out any prickly parts. Now cut in half from top to bottom and cut out the core. Slice the pineapple into bite-sized pieces.

Cut the bananas into medallions and mix all the fruit except the watermelon together in a large bowl. You can add the watermelon to the edge of the bowl for presentation— one wedge per service—and a wedge of lemon to squeeze over the honeydew and cantaloupe.

A splash of kirsch or peach brandy would make a nice finishing touch. You could also add some Prunes in Port (p. 187).

TWELVE

Beverages

COFFEE

I'll start this chapter with a few comments on coffee, since it is most often the opening act for breakfast. (Tea drinkers, please be patient.) I have used the same supplier for my coffee at Good Enough for twenty years. He delivers 100 percent Colombian coffee to me each week. As you might guess, we pour a lot of coffee, and our customers have always found it to be quite satisfactory.

Well, almost always. When the Starbucks craze swept the country, coffee bars became as numerous as pizza parlors in the city. People became accustomed to higher-priced, stronger, and I think, slightly bitter coffees. I started getting complaints at the restaurant that my coffee was "weak."

Tastes were changing. I remember the coffees that I drank in Belgium and France. It does seem that they were stronger, but I don't remember Europeans drinking so much of it as Americans do. Anyway, I spoke to my coffee man, and he was able to provide us with a darker roast, and that seems to have satisfied the coffee connoisseurs.

I have always believed that beyond the kind of coffee you use, the water, brewing method, and so on, the critical concern is how freshly brewed the coffee is. If coffee sits for 15 minutes on the heating plate, its taste will change markedly for the worse. Its aroma will change too, and a quick sniff will tell you that it has become "old." Throw it out and brew a fresh pot.

We received the automatic drip coffeemaker we use at home as a wedding gift in 1985. It still works! We use a gold filter basket to avoid using paper with each pot we make. Gold is the least reactive of all metals and so imparts no taste to the coffee. We've only had to replace our filter basket once, and think how many trees we've saved!

Wash your coffeemaker periodically by "brewing" a pot of water with a teaspoon of white vinegar in it. Follow by brewing a pot of plain water.

The water itself will affect the coffee. New York City is blessed with excellent water that harbors no noticeable tastes. If you live in an area where the water has a high mineral content or does have "tastes," try using bottled spring-water.

If you use one of those hourglass-shaped coffeemakers into which you pour boiling water, wait for 1 minute after the water has boiled before pouring it onto the coffee. Coffee should not be boiled. The same advice applies to the French press-style coffeemaker.

Once coffee is opened, it should be stored in a tightly covered container in the refrigerator. Coffee contains oils that are reactive to air.

If you grind your own beans, don't overgrind them or you'll get a dirty-looking sediment in the coffee. The grind should be grainy, not powdery.

I have never been quite able to figure out what the lines on the inside of the pot of my coffeemaker are supposed to mean. A measured cup of water reaches the number 2 line. The giant mugs we use at home contain 1½ cups of liquid. In the mornings I pour water to the number 7 line (3½ cups) and put 3 heaping scoops (about 6 tablespoons) of coffee into the filter basket. This satisfies the octane requirements of my husband and me for the morning. You'll want to play with your own ratios, depending on the type of coffee you're using and how strong you like it.

TEA

I am not an expert on teas, but I can discuss them briefly from the perspective of my own experience and preferences.

Basically, teas can be divided between the herbals, which are noncaffeine, and the caffeine teas. Everyone has a preference among the herbals: Rose hip tea contains vitamin C; chamomile tea has a calming effect; licorice and peppermint teas are stomach settling. So the stories go.

The caffeine teas include orange pekoe, black, green, and the blends. English breakfast tea is less aromatic than Earl Grey, and Earl Grey is less aromatic than Darjeeling. I am ignorant about oolong, although Mark Twain tells a story about its taking the longest time to be rid of!

The purported health benefits of tea over coffee tend to rise and fall like the barometer. The green teas served in Asian restaurants are currently in vogue, but they do contain caffeine. I have heard that black tea is superior to others in that it is supposed to be more healthful, or perhaps it is just less pernicious.

Personally, I have coffee during the day and a cup of licorice tea before going to bed. My husband has a cup of plain old Lipton's (a blend of black and orange pekoe) in the evening—he sweetens it with honey and it doesn't keep him from falling asleep when he wants to.

We use tea bags at the restaurant, little china teapots, and cups and saucers. I know from a former English boyfriend's mother that "proper" tea is made with loose tea and an infuser, that pot and teacups are warmed with hot water before steeping and pouring, that the tea must steep for 10 minutes, and that the milk and sugar are put in the cup before pouring out the tea. The proper teacup should have a thin lip and a handle. Pinky finger up is optional for men.

What the Japanese make of tea is something else again. Perhaps after the rigor of the tea ceremony, the tea that finally touches the lips is indeed transcendent. Although I have never participated in the tea ceremony, I did work with a brilliant Japanese chef at the Russian Tea Room and I was in awe of the skill and care-filled appreciation with which he worked. I know he understood the tea ceremony—you could just tell!

Chai

Makes 6 cups

Chai was supposedly devised in India as a way of making a palatable beverage out of low-quality tea. I was told that by an Indian gentleman of very slight acquaintance, so I don't know how reliable the story is. However it may be, chai has definitely made the scene in the States. It is quite delicious, wakes you up in the morning, and fills the house with a spicy aroma.

8 pods cardamom
2 tablespoons fresh ginger, peeled and grated
1 stick cinnamon
8 whole cloves
8 peppercorns
4 cups cold water
4 tablespoons black tea in an infuser (or 6 tea bags—
   Lipton's is fine)
1 cup milk
2 tablespoons sugar (or sweeten to taste)

Crack the cardamom pods with the flat part of a knife and combine with the ginger, cinnamon, cloves, peppercorns, and water in a medium pot. Let the spices soak for ½ hour.

Bring to a boil. Remove from the heat and add the tea. Let steep for 10 minutes.

Strain the liquid through a piece of cheesecloth, pressing it out of the spices and tea with a spoon. Return the liquid to the pot, discarding the solids, then add the milk and bring to a boil. Remove from heat and add the sugar to taste. Bring to a boil twice more with a minute cooling in between.

Serve hot in mugs or delicate china teacups!

Indian Spiced Coffee

Makes 4 cups

When I first had this coffee in 1991, I was told that it was called siddha *coffee, which translates as "saint's coffee." Try it and see if you think it's as enlightened a beverage as I do.*

1 cup water
1 cinnamon stick
8 cardamom pods, split
8 black peppercorns
¾ cup half-and-half
3 tablespoons sugar (or to taste)
2 cups strong, freshly brewed coffee
Pinch nutmeg (optional)

In a medium-sized pot bring the water to a boil and add the cinnamon, cardamom, and peppercorns. Bring to a second boil, reduce, and simmer for 5 minutes.

Add the half-and-half and sugar and stir. Add the coffee and raise the heat to bring just under a boil. Remove from the heat, strain the liquid, and discard the solids.

Serve right away with a sprinkle of nutmeg. Indian Spiced Coffee also makes an excellent iced drink.

Angel's Cocoa

Makes 4 cups

Our good friend Miguel Angel Medina is the oldest of seven children. He was the family's official cocoa maker, and this is his recipe. Callebaut cocoa is very rich; if you use another brand, you will probably need more cocoa.

2 cups water
Pinch salt
8 tablespoons sugar
4 tablespoons unsweetened cocoa (Callebaut is the best!)
2½ cups half-and-half
1 teaspoon pure vanilla extract

Put the water and the salt into a medium-sized pot over a low heat. Add the sugar and cocoa, stir to dissolve, and heat for 10 minutes.

Turn the heat up to medium and add the half-and-half. Stir constantly, letting the cocoa get quite hot but not boiling. In the last 2 minutes add the vanilla.

Serve with a few of those little marshmallows, if you like.

For Mocha Java combine Angel's cocoa and hot coffee in equal amounts.

Ginger-Honey Tonic

Makes 1½ cups of concentrate

Feeling a bit dyspeptic? Dank and gloomy in head and heart? Try Dr. Carrie's Universal Ginger-Honey Tonic and bring sunny skies back into your day!

3 cups water
1 heaping tablespoon peeled, chopped ginger
½ teaspoon cayenne
Juice of ½ lemon
Honey

Put everything except honey into a medium pot and bring to a boil. Reduce by ½ to about 1½ cups. Let cool and strain out solids. Tonic concentrate can be stored in the refrigerator for up to 3 weeks.

For serving, heat ¼ cup tonic with 1½ cups of water. Pour into cups and stir in honey to sweeten.

Virgin Mary

Makes 1 drink

This is a tangy stabilizer for a system that may have had an evening of some gastric turmoil. You can easily convert the Virgin to a Magdalene with a shot of vodka.

6 ounces cold tomato juice
1 tablespoon beef bouillon
1 teaspoon Worcestershire sauce
½ teaspoon horseradish
Pinch celery salt
Pinch black pepper
Lemon wedge
Celery stalk (optional)

Mix first six ingredients together in an 8-ounce glass. Squeeze in the lemon wedge and stir. Add a couple of ice cubes and the stalk of celery.

Hangover Remedy

Makes 2 servings

This formula predates Prohibition, and besides that, it's all natural! If the raw egg worries you, skip the recipe in favor of an Alka-Selzer. But remember, Rocky drank eight of them and he became champion of the world!

1½ cups **Fresh Samantha Veggie Cha Cha, or tomato juice**
1 **raw egg**
3 **drops Tabasco**
Dash of Worcestershire sauce
Pinch black pepper
2 **wedges of lemon**

Combine all ingredients except the lemon in a blender for about 5 seconds. Serve in glasses with a lemon wedge. Down the hatch!

Protein Shake

Makes 1 serving

Whether you're off red meat or trying to beef up at the gym, here's a tasty way of supplementing your protein intake. Dense fruits like bananas are a good base for making supplemental powders palatable.

1 banana
½ cup pineapple chunks
⅓ mango
Vegetable protein powder (according to directions)
½ cup orange juice
3 ice cubes

Blend the fruits until smooth. Add the protein powder and blend. Add the orange juice, blend, and add the ice and blend until pulverized. Serve immediately.

Nondairy Shake

Makes 1 serving

This is a variation of the Protein Shake. Soy milk is an excellent source of calcium and protein for anyone who has a problem digesting milk.

1 banana
5 ripe strawberries
½ cup pineapple chunks
½ cup soy milk
1 to 2 tablespoons honey
½ cup orange juice

Blend the fruits, soy milk, and honey until smooth, then blend in the orange juice. Start the blender at a low speed at first, then increase speed. Serve immediately—a fruit shake has a tendency to separate if allowed to sit. If this happens, just give it another turn in the blender.

Edgar's Almond-Coconut Collins

Makes 2 drinks

I don't know who "Edgar" is. Maybe it's Edgar Cayce, the psychic healer who said that eating three almonds a day will keep you from getting cancer. Don't quote me on that, and don't send me any of your doctor bills. This drink is very rich and delicious—that much I know for sure.

½ cup grated coconut, loosely packed
½ cup slivered almonds
2 tablespoons Coco Lopez Cream of Coconut
1 tablespoon honey
1 cup orange juice
1 teaspoon cinnamon
1½ cups cold soy milk
3 ice cubes
Ground nutmeg for serving

Blend all ingredients except nutmeg at low speed until the nuts and ice are completely pulverized and the drink is thick and smooth. Serve immediately in a tall glass with a sprinkle of nutmeg.

Fruit Smoothie

Makes 1 drink

I took a crash course in smoothies from Masa, the owner of the Euphoria Café, around the corner from Good Enough to Eat. Thanks, Masa!

½ cup milk
¼ cup blueberries
5 ripe strawberries
¼ mango (a few slices)
1 banana
½ cup plain yogurt

Combine in a blender until fruit is pulverized and drink is thick and smooth. Serve immediately.

Pineapple-Kiwi Smoothie

Makes 2 drinks

*M*y oldest son, Bucko, put on his lab coat and worked out the proportions for this smoothie. This was experimental batch number 3.

½ cup milk
½ cup yogurt
1½ tablespoons honey
1 kiwi fruit, peeled, cut in half
1 cup pineapple chunks
⅓ cup grated coconut
⅓ mango (three slices)
2 ice cubes

Blend all ingredients at low speed until thick and smooth.

Coconut-Grapefruit Smoothie

Makes 1 to 2 drinks

The yogurt and the grapefruit juice blend quite nicely, but I wouldn't let the drink sit around too long—it might take on a perplexing texture.

1 tablespoon Coco Lopez Cream of Coconut
½ cup grated fresh coconut (or ⅓ cup store-bought
　unsweetened coconut)
1 banana
⅓ mango, peeled and sliced
½ cup plain yogurt
1 cup grapefruit juice

Blend the coconut cream, coconut, and banana until smooth. Add the mango and yogurt and blend until the mango is pulverized. Add the grapefruit juice and blend. Serve immediately.

Pink Cherry Lemonade

Makes 2 quarts

This recipe won first prize in Cheers *magazine as a chaser for chilled vodka.*

5 cups water
½ cup sugar, or to taste
2 cups fresh lemon juice
2 cups frozen sour cherries (defrosted, drained)
Cherries on the stem for garnish
Lime wedges for garnish

Heat 1 cup of the water and dissolve the sugar in it. Pour into a large pitcher and add the rest of the water, lemon juice, and cherries. Mash a few of the cherries for color, stir well, and serve as an iced drink with a cherry and a lime wedge.

Notes:

❤ Use as basis for Tom or Vodka Collins

❤ Substitute frozen blueberries for cherries for Blue Lemonade. Well, it won't really be blue—only food coloring will do that!

❤ Honey can be used in place of sugar. Dissolve in hot, but never boiling, water.

Papa's Juice

Makes 2½ quarts

My *boys call their father Papa. They used to call me Mama until Bucko started taking Latin in the eighth grade. Now all the boys are calling me Mater. Everyone else in the family has a nickname: Asa is "Buddha," Conner is "Buster," Buck is either "Bucko" or "Buckaroo," and Bill (alias Papa) calls me Bub (the u sounds like the oo in took). Their grandfather and grandmother (my parents) are called Noo-noo and Goo-goo, respectively. My brother, Douglas Levin, who founded the Fresh Samantha Juice Company, is called Uncle Oogie. All that is cute, I suppose, but you can't eat it.*

Papa has made this juice for the boys for as long as I can remember, and they never tire of it. When they have friends over, they always ask for some of Papa's Juice. Bill read somewhere that if kids are drinking a lot of juice to quench their thirst, they're probably getting too much acid in their stomachs, so he cuts the juice with water. It's very easy to make.

4 cups orange juice (no pulp—kids don't like it!)
4 cups cranberry juice
2 cups water

We use one of those gallon-sized cranberry juice bottles with the handle as a container.

Combine the orange juice, cranberry juice, and water in your container. (It's a 4:1 ratio of juice to water, if you want to make a smaller amount.) That's all there is to it! Bill has found that if he doesn't stick to this ratio, the boys notice and complain. Don't mess with success!

THIRTEEN

Brunch

I think it was in 1999, a year prior to writing this book, that I had a telephone interview with William Grimes, the food critic of the *New York Times*. He was researching an article on brunch and said that I was one of the few chefs working in a restaurant that had anything to say about it. I don't know how many chefs he spoke to subsequent to our conversation, or who the others of the "few" might have been, but it started me thinking.

The weekend, daylight-long phenomenon that gets its name by amalgamating *breakfast* and *lunch* that has become such an event in the city (New York, as well as many others)—why would chefs have so little to say about it? Why was it a topic that I could easily rattle on about?

My theory is that most chefs whose opinions might be judged newsworthy stay up late nights as maestros of the evening meal, which has always been the brightest feather in the *toque blanche*. They're just not up early enough to take a serious interest in brunch.

I believe that the difference between me and them, or to put it another way, between my restaurant and their restaurants, is that Good Enough to Eat was built on breakfast. It is literally famous for it. Even twenty years ago when I first opened, there were lines outside for the weekend brunch, and they are still there, thank God. For a long time, our very excellent dinner menu was obscured by the glare of our daytime success—no longer the case, I'm happy to say.

Besides brunch's being a testament to my early and continuing obsession with breakfast food, I'm a mother—I can't stay up late! You men, even the fathers among you, can still get away with that. So, really, I don't blame you for not having much to say about brunch. Really!

The irony about our huge brunch business is that it isn't brunch at all. It's a very festive daylong meal drawn almost exclusively from our extensive breakfast menu. There are a couple of specials, I'll admit, but for the most part it's the same menu we serve every day from 8:00 A.M. to 4:00 P.M.! Egad! I hope my customers don't feel swindled.

I include a few special recipes in this chapter, but we will be composing brunches around certain themes, using recipes already at your disposal in other parts of the book. You are certainly encouraged to daub up your own compositions, with the recipes as your palette of colors.

Weekend at the Lake with Sautéed Cornmeal Trout

Serves 4

You can trudge back from a predawn fishing excursion with a mess of trout or buy them as fresh as you can from your fishmonger. Either way, this menu will work.

SAUTÉED CORNMEAL TROUT
BRAISED TOMATOES, PAGE 186
SCRAMBLED EGGS, PAGE 9
ENGLISH MUFFINS, PAGE 129
HONEYDEW MELON SLICES
LEMON WEDGES
COFFEE OR TEA
ICED BOTTLE OF RIESLING OR GEWÜRZTRAMINER

Sautéed Cornmeal Trout

¾ cup coarse yellow cornmeal
1 teaspoon kosher salt
½ teaspoon cracked black pepper
½ teaspoon paprika
⅓ cup milk
4 fillets of trout
1 tablespoon butter
1 teaspoon vegetable oil

Mix the dry ingredients together on a plate. Put the milk in a medium-sized bowl. Have a second plate ready for the fish.

If you have just caught the fish, the skin will be tight and the flesh firm and slightly translucent, certainly not white. Look for these characteristics when you buy fish.

Dip the fillet in the milk with one hand and coat with the dry ingredients with the other hand, then put on the second plate. If you're not going to cook right away, store the fillets in the refrigerator.

Get part of the butter and oil very hot in your frying pan before you put in the fish. You're supposed to cook fish 10 minutes per inch of thickness. Following that rule, you cook the fillets 3 to 5 minutes per side. The fillets should have some room, so unless your pan is very large, I'd say cook two at a time. Keep the pan moving over the heat to prevent sticking. Add a little more butter and oil and get it hot before the second batch.

Keep the trout hot in a 200-degree oven while you make the scrambled eggs.

If you have a broiler in your lakeside cottage, the tomatoes—which you will have prepared ahead of time—will take about 7 minutes, so they should go under the broiler a couple of minutes after the trout goes in the pan. If using the oven for the tomatoes, you need 15 minutes. Put them in 5 minutes before the trout!

The English Muffins just need to be toasted. You made them yesterday, remember? The honeydew is sliced. A lemon will give you 8 wedges—cut off the ends, slice the wedges, cut off the pith on the inner edge, and pick out the seeds with the point of the knife. Serve lemon with the melon and the trout.

The coffee is ready. The wine is chilled. Enjoy!

Midnight Brunch for Two with Israeli Couscous

*H*ere's a late-night repast for lovebirds. Let's suppose he made most of it the night before. It pays to be prepared, as every good scout knows.

ISRAELI COUSCOUS
CAVIAR OR LUMPFISH
SMOKED SALMON WITH POACHED EGGS AND CRÈME FRAÎCHE
CHOCOLATE BREAD PUDDING
STRAWBERRIES
CHAMPAGNE

Pinch salt plus 1 teaspoon for the pot
2 lemons (1 for zest and juice; 1 for slices)
¾ cup Israeli couscous (at most gourmet food stores and many supermarkets)
¼ teaspoon cracked black pepper
Pinch red pepper flakes
2 tablespoons virgin olive oil
2 tablespoon finely chopped red onion, plus some slices for garnish
2 tablespoons chopped fresh dill
2 tablespoons plus 1 teaspoon caviar or black lumpfish
¼ pound Scottish smoked salmon (4 slices)—get the good stuff!
4 eggs
2 teaspoons Mock Crème Fraîche (p. 189)
2 teaspoons snipped chives (optional decoration)

Prepare the Chocolate Bread Pudding the day before by soaking some Cocoa-Chocolate Bread (p. 103) in some Fundamental French Toast custard (p. 61). Put about 5 to 6 cups of the soaked bread into a buttered 9 x 9-inch baking dish. Bake for 25 to 30 minutes at 350 degrees. Let cool before refrigerating.

About one hour before midnight, take inventory and make sure you're ready to go. The champagne is on ice. The pudding is in the fridge. Crème fraîche in the fridge. And so on . . . check, check.

Fill a 2½-quart pot half full of water and add the 1 teaspoon of salt and bring to a boil. Zest one of the lemons. Reserve the zest and strain half of the juice of the zested lemon into the boiling water. Add the couscous. Cook for 7 minutes. Drain, rinse under cool water, and reserve in a bowl.

When you put the couscous in, put the pinch of salt, pepper, and red pepper flakes into a frying pan with the olive oil and sauté for 1 minute over medium heat. Add the chopped onion to the pan and cook for another minute, deglazing with some lemon juice. Take off the heat and add to the bowl of couscous, along with the dill and lemon zest.

Bring water plus a drop of white vinegar to just under a boil for poaching the eggs in either the frying pan (you need not clean it) or a pot (see Poached Eggs, p. 28).

Add the 2 tablespoons of caviar to the couscous mix and plate for 2 servings. Place 2 slices of smoked salmon over each serving of couscous.

Proceed to poach your eggs following the Poached Eggs technique. Remove with a slotted spoon, catching excess water by holding a paper towel against the bottom of the spoon. Place the eggs on top of the salmon.

Place a dollop of crème fraîche on top of each egg yolk, sprinkle the teaspoon caviar over them, and snip some chives over the lot. Serve with some slices of lemon and onion on the side of the plates.

Have some fresh ripe strawberries cut in half lengthwise, with the caps still on, in a dish with some more crème fraîche nearby on the table. Pop the champagne.

Serve a wedge of Chocolate Bread Pudding with the last of the champagne for dessert.

If you pull this off with panache, it's *amóre* for sure.

Just Family

In my house Bill and I get up at 6:15 A.M., have breakfast at 7:00 A.M., and leave the house by 7:30 in order to get the boys to school by 8:00. But when we visit my parents in Connecticut for a weekend, we get up a lot later—around nine o'clock.

The Saturday-morning breakfast is always the same: French toast, fried eggs, bacon, white toast, orange juice, and coffee. It's undoubtedly a regression to childhood that I always find this dependable breakfast comforting.

FRENCH TOAST MADE WITH WHITE BREAD, PAGES 61 AND 86

BACON, PAGE 163

FRIED EGGS, PAGE 24

CRACQUELIN TOAST, PAGE 96

PRUNE DANISH, PAGE 147

PAPA'S JUICE, PAGE 207, OR UNCLE OOGIE'S SUPER JUICE

COFFEE OR TEA

If you have exhausted yourself the day before, making the Cracquelin and Danish, you can use a good-quality white bread from the store for the French toast. Remember why the French call it *pain perdu*— the bread is best when it's a little stale.

The Cracquelin can be toasted under the broiler, if the slices are too thick for the toaster. The Danish can be warmed for 10 minutes in a 200-degree oven.

The bacon should go on first, then the French toast, and lastly, the eggs. Save a tad of the bacon fat to mix with the butter for the eggs. Don't worry—cholesterol is a necessary component of brain cells!

Buddha (Asa) loves Fresh Samantha Super Juice, but there are lots of other good ones from Uncle Oogie. Papa's Juice is always a hit.

Serve this exact breakfast to your family every Saturday morning for six months straight and see how comforting it becomes. (Just a suggestion!)

Autumn in the Park

Let's say the leaves are just starting to turn, the sweaters are coming out of the cedar chest, the birds are dodging the footballs flying through the air, pumpkins are in the markets, and there's a free Saturday afternoon concert in the outdoor ampitheater. Time to pack the hamper, pick up the kids from soccer, and tote a picnic to the park.

Let's also say you've got a bit of baked ham (or roast turkey or chicken) in the fridge, some Savory Scones tucked away in the freezer, and you'd decided to make some Chocolate Doughnuts first thing that morning. What's left on the shopping list? Apples, blueberries, strawberries, bananas, eggs, broccoli, tomatoes, vanilla ice cream, and yogurt.

BAKED HAM ON SAVORY SCONES, PAGES 175 AND 119
BROCCOLI SLAW, PAGE 181
HARD-BOILED EGGS, PAGE 29
TOMATOES
FRUIT SALAD WITH APPLES, STRAWBERRIES, BLUEBERRIES,
AND BANANAS
CHOCOLATE DOUGHNUTS, PAGE 144
YOGURT AND VANILLA ICE CREAM CRÈME FRAÎCHE, PAGE 189
ANGEL'S COCOA, PAGE 200

The Chocolate Doughnuts should be done by now.

Defrost the scones by putting them into a 200-degree oven for 20 minutes. Cut them for sandwiches, which you make with some baked ham.

Hard-boil some eggs and let them cool to peel at the park. Make the Broccoli Slaw. Wash the tomatoes and cut out the stem cores—slice at the park. Wash all the fruit. Peel, core, and slice the apples, layer them at the bottom of a plastic container that has a fitted lid, and squeeze some lemon juice over them. Cut out the caps and stem cores of the strawberries, slice them in half lengthwise, and layer them on top of the apples. Put the blueberries on top. (You could do the fruit the night before. It will store quite well in the refrigerator, layered in a covered container. Don't add the bananas until the next day, preferably just before serving.)

Whip the yogurt and the ice cream together to make a crème fraîche topping or dip for the fruit and/or doughnuts. Put it in a covered plastic container in the refrigerator until you are ready to go.

Make a quart of Angel's Cocoa and put it in a thermos just before leaving. Pack up everything. Don't forget the hot cups, plates, forks, spoons, napkins, a bag for garbage, some mustard and mayonnaise, salt for the eggs and tomatoes, a folding knife to cut the tomatoes and bananas, and the blanket.

Note: If you would prefer, substitute hot apple cider for the cocoa. Simmer 1 quart of apple cider for 25 minutes with a stick of cinnamon and 3 whole cloves. Remove the cinnamon and cloves, skim the cinnamon scum, and pour into the thermos.

Veggie Brunch

I'll bet your carnivorous friends and neighbors won't even notice that the meat is missing. And for the ovophobes, guess what? No eggs!

Most vegetarians that I know are quite inventive and willing to expend extra effort in entertaining their palates. This menu requires advance planning and certainly effort. I hope you find it imaginative as well.

RATATOUILLE TURNOVERS, PAGE 185

SCRAMBLED TOFU, PAGE 16

7-GRAIN BREAD, PAGE 91

EGGLESS SCONES WITH RAISINS AND MINT, PAGE 121

APRICOT COMPOTE, PAGE 160 OR PEACH-GINGER PRESERVES, PAGE 157

VEGETARIAN CHORIZO, PAGE 182

KIWI-BANANA-LIME FRUIT SALAD

SELECTION OF HERBAL TEAS (CHAMOMILE, ROSE HIPS, PEPPER-MINT)

CHAI, PAGE 198

COFFEE

If you're planning a weekend event, the only things you want to prepare on the morning of the big day are the Scrambled Tofu, scones, and fruit salad. The compote or the preserves could be in the refrigerator for a month, so we'll count on that being available when needed. The Ratatouille Turnovers could have been prepared a week ahead of time and frozen, uncooked, in their pastry shells. The chorizos should be prepared Thursday morning prior to a Saturday brunch and stored in the refrigerator until you're ready to cook them. The 7-Grain Bread should be made the day before so that it is fresh.

Review the recipe for Scrambled Tofu. Have everything prepped ahead of time so you can jump right into the cooking.

Preheat the oven to 350 degrees.

Following the recipe for Eggless Scones on page 121; get them ready and in the oven. If you've made the 3-inch turnovers, you can put them in the oven right out of the freezer at the same time as the scones. They will take about the same amount of time to bake. The 7-inch turnovers will take about 30 minutes at 350 degrees. Skip the egg wash glaze in deference to oviphobes.

Start the Chai about 1 hour before your guests are due to arrive. Ladle out from the pot.

Peel and slice kiwis and bananas. Put them in a bowl and squeeze some fresh lime over the fruit. Your fruit salad is ready for the table.

Put the 7-Grain Bread on the table with a couple of slices already cut and point the way to the toaster. Have some butter and compote or preserves in the neighborhood of the bread.

Brew the coffee.

Arrange the scones and turnovers on plates and place on the table.

Cook the chorizo and keep warm to serve with the Scrambled Tofu, which you should prepare to order.

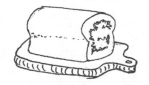

Graduation Day Brunch

Every year in June after the academic caps have been flung, we get sizable parties of recent graduates from the high schools in the city. This is a menu composed of what the celebrants seem to prefer. If you'll notice, it's pretty sweet—just like they are! If your party is coming with college diplomas, you might want to fix omelettes instead of scrambled. They get sophisticated in college.

PETER PAUL PANCAKES, PAGE 41

SCRAMBLED EGGS, PAGE 9

GRANOLA WITH FRESH BLUEBERRIES AND STRAWBERRIES, PAGE 71

BACON, PAGE 163

PORK SAUSAGE, PAGE 165

BLUEBERRY MUFFINS (2 CUPS OF BLUEBERRIES INSTEAD OF
PEACHES AND MANGOES), PAGE 106

GOOD ENOUGH TO EAT BISCUITS, PAGE 125

STRAWBERRY BUTTER, PAGE 126

STRAWBERRY JAM, PAGE 154

COFFEE

TEA

ORANGE JUICE

PINK CHERRY LEMONADE, PAGE 206

A lot of this can be made ahead of time, and should be, because you want to have a lot of time to lavish on your new graduate.

You'll have a sack of Granola in the pantry, biscuits in the freezer, Strawberry Butter and some jam in the fridge.

Start the blueberry muffins about an hour or so before your valedictorian is due to arrive. They take 25 minutes in the oven. After the muffins are out, lower the heat to 200 and put the biscuits in right out of the freezer for 15 minutes.

Prepare the pancake batter so that you can cook them along with the scrambled eggs à la minute.

The Granola can be put on the table with spoons, bowls, berries, and milk alongside for self service. The muffins can be pyramided on a plate and set on the table next to the biscuits, Strawberry Butter, and jam. Have small plates and knives available.

Time the coffee brewing so it's as fresh as possible. Have the lemonade and O.J. chilled. Make sure there's hot water for the tea.

Cook the bacon and sausage and keep it warm over the stove or in the oven.

When the grads arrive, you'll have to apprise them of the availability of Peter Paul Pancakes and the scrambled eggs, or else they'll fill up on muffins. You can either take orders (grads like that!) or shanghai them to the stove to be on hand to receive their order.

Just think, soon they'll be off to college and all you'll have to do is pay bills!

Mother's Day Brunch

Serves 1 mother

Here's my own fantasy brunch, served to me in bed, late in the morning, so that I can eat it while I watch my favorite group of political pundits shout at each other on TV.

The boys will have to get up early to help, and Bill will have a chance to cook some of the recipes he's been helping me write about. This year (2001) Mother's Day falls on Sunday, May 13. Thirteen is my lucky number—maybe I'll get lucky!

SPINACH-SALAMI-COMTÉ OMELETTE, PAGE 22
PRUNE DANISH, PAGE 147
STRAWBERRIES WITH CRÈME FRAÎCHE, PAGE 189
INDIAN SPICED COFFEE, PAGE 199

Everything has to be made early that morning before I wake up. Thank you very much.

Father's Day Brunch

Serves 1 father

To be fair, I had to ask my husband what he would like me to make for his Father's Day breakfast. This, then, is the menu he gave me. He knows my food very well, so you dads can trust his choices. I do think, however, that some of them come from an appetite for revenge for getting him to make Prune Danish for me.

BUCKWHEAT PANCAKES WITH CHUNKY APPLE SAUCE
AND SOUR CREAM, PAGE 44 AND PAGE 45
FRIED EGGS, PAGE 24
BACON, PAGE 163
SOUR CREAM COFFEE CAKE WITH CRUMB TOPPING, PAGE 132
BLUEBERRIES WITH CREAM
COFFEE

If you check the recipe, you'll see that I have to start the Buckwheat Pancakes the night before. Once the batter is ready, I can quickly make the pancakes on the griddle after the bacon is done.

Okay, but first I have to work on the coffee cake. Three elements to that: streusel, cake, and topping. I'll make the streusel and the cake, put the cake in the oven, and make the Chunky Apple Sauce. The applesauce should be done at about the same time I have to put the crumb topping on the cake.

Once the coffee cake comes out of the oven, it needs to cool. He'll smell the coffee cake! I'll give him some blueberries with a little cream and a sprinkle of sugar and a cup of coffee to keep him busy while I fry the eggs over-easy in the frying pan and cook the pancakes on the griddle.

Just when he's finished the blueberries, I'll be able to deliver a plate with two Buckwheat Pancakes with a dollop of sour cream, applesauce, and maple syrup, and piled up alongside of that: two eggs, two pieces of bacon, and a slice of warm Sour Cream Coffee Cake. Then a big *bisou*, and I'll offer to get him some more coffee. Easy! And only once a year—what a bargain!

New Year's Day Brunch

New Year's is one of the busiest days of the year at Good Enough to Eat. People start pouring in the minute we open at 10:00 A.M. and keep coming in a steady stream until we shut the brunch down at 4:00 P.M. The early birds frequently still have their party clothes on—coteries of rumpled tuxes and party dresses. The bar is kept busy with Bloody Marys, champagne (more, yet!), and shooters of Hangover Remedy.

However we may be occupied assisting the prior night's cele-brants recover their equilibrium, here's a menu for those of us who are feeding friends and family on New Year's Day. You'll notice that it assumes quite a few prior adventures with my book.

CINNAMON-SWIRL FRENCH TOAST WITH PEAR-CRANBERRY
TOPPING, PAGE 64 AND PAGE 62
BACON, PAGE 163
SMOKED SALMON PLATTER WITH WHOLE-WHEAT TOAST, PAGE 89
MINISCONES, PAGE 115, WITH ORANGE-BOURBON
MARMALADE, PAGE 158
SWEET POTATO BISCUITS, PAGE 128 WITH HAM, PAGE 175 AND
CRANBERRY JAM, PAGE 156
TRICOLOR CRISPY NACHOS WITH SALSA, SOUR CREAM,
AND EGGS, PAGE 14
PERFECT CINNAMON BUNS, PAGE 137
MIMOSAS, HARD APPLE CIDER, AND VIRGIN MARYS, PAGE 201
ORANGE AND GRAPEFRUIT JUICES
COFFEE AND TEA

Note: For Miniscones, use the recipe on page 115: Instead of dividing the dough into 2 balls, divide into 4 balls and cut into 16 triangles. Bake for about 15 minutes.

These are the recipes you need to have prepared in the last few days or weeks of the prior year: Orange-Bourbon Mar-malade, Cranberry Jam, Pear-Cranberry Topping, salsa, miniscones and Sweet Potato Biscuits (in the freezer). The

Cinnamon-Swirl Bread can be a couple of days old for the French toast, but the Whole-Wheat Bread should be made the night before.

The list for the Smoked Salmon Platter includes 1 slice per guest of high-quality smoked salmon, chopped red onion, capers, crumbled hard-boiled egg, cream cheese, butter, and lemon wedges. Put the platter together so that each guest can build his own canapé on a Whole-Wheat Toast triangle.

The cinnamon buns take about 2 hours, so they need to be started early.

Perhaps you have some Glazed Baked Ham (p. 175) left over from the holidays. Cut it into bite-sized slices to fit on the Sweet Potato Biscuits. Once the cinnamon buns are out of the oven, let the oven cool down to 200 degrees. Both the biscuits and the scones will heat up in 15 minutes in the oven at that temperature. Arrange the ham, Sweet Potato Biscuits, and Cranberry Jam together. The scones should be with the Orange-Bourbon Marmalade. Butter and mustard should be available.

At home I have a griddle, so after the bacon is done, I can use the griddle to cook the Cinnamon-Swirl French Toast and make the nacho eggs in a frying pan. Serve the French Toast with maple syrup, bacon, and some Pear-Cranberry Topping on the side. The eggs are served with the salsa and sour cream, and some bacon as well.

You probably want to set up a bar area with a pitcher of Virgin Marys, champagne and orange juice (to mix half-and-half) for Mimosas, chilled hard apple cider, grapefruit juice, coffee, tea, and perhaps a bottle of vodka.

Don't forget to put the cinnamon buns on the table while they're still warm.

Have a great New Year!

❖❖❖❖❖❖ BIBLIOGRAPHY ❖❖❖❖❖❖

Beard, James. *Beard on Bread*. New York: Knopf, 1973.

Bourdain, Anthony. *Kitchen Confidential*. New York: Harper Collins, 2000.

Child, Julia, with Dorie Greenspan. *Baking with Julia*. New York: William Morrow, 1996.

Cunningham, Marion. *The Breakfast Book*. New York: Knopf, 1987.

Cunningham, Marion. *The Fannie Farmer Baking Book*. New York: Knopf, 1984.

De Gouy, Louis P. *The Gold Cookbook*. New York: Greenberg, 1947.

Dedouaire, Robert. *Aux Delices de ses Dames, La Renaissance de la Patisserie Wallone*. 1985.

Levin, Carrie, and Ann Nickinson. *Good Enough to Eat: Bountiful Home Cooking*. New York: Simon and Schuster, 1987.

Mathiot, Ginette, and Lionel Poilâne. *Pain, Cuisine et Gourmandises*, Paris: Albin Michel, 1985.

Pillsbury, Ann. *Ann Pillsbury's Baking Book*. New York: Pocket, 1950.

Rombauer, Irma S., and Marion Rombauer Becker. *Joy of Cooking*. New York: Plume, 1997.

Scherber, Amy. *Amy's Bread*. New York: William Morrow, 1996.

Shank, Dorothy. *Magic Chef Cooking*. St. Louis: American Stove Company, 1934.

Small, Marvin, ed. *The World's Best Recipes*. New York: Pocket, 1957.

Wakefield, Ruth. *Toll House Tried and True Recipes*. New York: Barrows, 1948.

INDEX